A First Course in Statistical Programming with R

This is the only introduction you'll need to start programming in R, the open-source language that is free to download, and lets you adapt the source code for your own requirements. Co-written by one of the R core development team, and by an established R author, this book comes with real R code that complies with the standards of the language.

Unlike other introductory books on the ground-breaking R system, this book emphasizes programming, including the principles that apply to most computing languages, and the techniques used to develop more complex projects. Learning the language is made easier by the frequent exercises within chapters which enable you to progress confidently through the book. More substantial exercises at the ends of chapters help to test your understanding.

Solutions, datasets, and any errata will be available from the book's website.

W. John Braun is an Associate Professor in the Department of Statistical and Actuarial Sciences at the University of Western Ontario. He is also a co-author, with John Maindonald, of *Data Analysis and Graphics Using R*.

Duncan J. Murdoch is an Associate Professor in the Department of Statistical and Actuarial Sciences at the University of Western Ontario. He was columnist and column editor of the statistical computing column of *Chance* during 1999–2000.

A First Course in
Statistical Programming
with R

W. John Braun and Duncan J. Murdoch

CAMBRIDGE
UNIVERSITY PRESS

CAMBRIDGE UNIVERSITY PRESS
Cambridge, New York, Melbourne, Madrid, Cape Town, Singapore, São Paulo, Delhi

Cambridge University Press
The Edinburgh Building, Cambridge CB2 8RU, UK

Published in the United States of America by Cambridge University Press, New York

www.cambridge.org
Information on this title: www.cambridge.org/9780521872652

First published 2007
Third printing with corrections 2008

Printed in the United Kingdom at the University Press, Cambridge

A catalogue record for this publication is available from the British Library

ISBN 978-0-521-87265-2 hardback
ISBN 978-0-521-69424-7 paperback

Contents

web sites 3,4

Preface

17 April 2012

This text began as notes for a course in statistical computing for second year actuarial and statistical students at the University of Western Ontario. Both authors are interested in statistical computing, both as support for our other research and for its own sake. However, we have found that our students were not learning the right sort of programming basics before they took our classes. At every level from undergraduate through Ph.D., we found that students were not able to produce simple, reliable programs; that they didn't understand enough about numerical computation to understand how rounding error could influence their results; and that they didn't know how to begin a difficult computational project.

We looked into service courses from other departments, but we found that they emphasized languages and concepts that our students would not use again. Our students need to be comfortable with simple programming so that they can put together a simulation of a stochastic model; they also need to know enough about numerical analysis so that they can do numerical computations reliably. We were unable to find this mix in an existing course, so we designed our own.

We chose to base this text on R. R is an open-source computing package which has seen a huge growth in popularity in the last few years. Being open source, it is easily obtainable by students and economical to install in our computing lab. One of us (Murdoch) is a member of the R core development team, and the other (Braun) is a co-author of a book on data analysis using R. These facts made it easy for us to choose R, but we are both strong believers in the idea that there are certain universals of programming, and in this text we try to emphasize those: it is not a manual about programming in R, it is a course in statistical programming that uses R.

Students starting this course are not assumed to have any programming experience or advanced statistical knowledge. They should be familiar with university-level calculus, and should have had exposure to a course in introductory probability, though that could be taken concurrently: the probabilistic concepts start in Chapter 5. (We include a concise appendix reviewing the probabilistic material.) We include some advanced topics in simulation, linear algebra, and optimization that an instructor may choose to skip in a one-semester course offering.

We have a lot of people to thank for their help in writing this book. The students in Statistical Sciences 259b have provided motivation and feedback, Lutong Zhou drafted several figures, and Diana Gillooly of Cambridge University Press, Professor Brian Ripley of Oxford University, and some anonymous reviewers all provided helpful suggestions. And of course, this book could not exist without R, and R would be far less valuable without the contributions of the worldwide R community.

Getting started

Welcome to the world of statistical programming. This book will contain a lot of specific advice about the hows and whys of the subject. We start in this chapter by giving you an idea of what statistical programming is all about. We will also tell you what to expect as you proceed through the rest of the book. The chapter will finish with some instructions about how to download and install R, the software package and language on which we base our programming examples.

1.1 What is statistical programming?

Computer programming involves controlling computers, telling them what calculations to do, what to display, etc. Statistical programming is harder to define. One definition might be that it's the kind of computer programming statisticians do – but statisticians do all sorts of programming. Another would be that it's the kind of programming one does when one is doing statistics – but again, statistics involves a wide variety of computing tasks.

For example, statisticians are concerned with collecting and analyzing data, and some statisticians would be involved in setting up connections between computers and laboratory instruments – but we would not call that statistical programming. Statisticians often oversee data entry from questionnaires, and may set up programs to aid in detecting data entry errors. That *is* statistical programming, but it is quite specialized, and beyond the scope of this book.

Statistical programming involves doing computations to aid in statistical analysis. For example, data must be summarized and displayed. Models must be fit to data, and the results displayed. These tasks can be done in a number of different computer applications: Microsoft Excel, SAS, SPSS, S-PLUS, R, Stata, etc. Using these applications is certainly statistical computing, and usually involves statistical programming, but it is not the focus of this book. In this book our aim is to provide a foundation for an understanding of how these applications work: we describe the calculations they do, and how you could do them yourself.

Since graphs play an important role in statistical analysis, drawing graphics of one, two, or higher dimensional data is an aspect of statistical programming.

An important part of statistical programming is stochastic simulation. Digital computers are naturally very good at exact, reproducible computations, but the real world is full of randomness. In stochastic simulation we program a computer to act as though it is producing random results, even though if we knew enough, the results would be exactly predictable.

Statistical programming is closely related to other forms of numerical programming. It involves optimization and approximation of mathematical functions. There is less emphasis on differential equations than in physics or applied mathematics (though this is slowly changing). We tend to place more of an emphasis on the results and less on the analysis of the algorithms than in computer science.

1.2 | Outline of the book

This book is an introduction to statistical programming. We will start with basic programming: how to tell a computer what to do. We do this using the open source R statistical package, so we will teach you R, but we will try not to *just* teach you R. We will emphasize those things that are common to many computing platforms.

Statisticians need to display data. We will show you how to construct statistical graphics. In doing this, we will learn a little bit about human vision, and how it motivates our choice of display.

In our introduction to programming, we will show how to control the flow of execution of a program. For example, we might wish to do repeated calculations as long as the input consists of positive integers, but then stop when an input value hits 0. Programming a computer requires basic logic, and we will touch on Boolean algebra, a formal way to manipulate logical statements. The best programs are thought through carefully *before* being implemented, and we will discuss how to break down complex problems into simple parts. When we are discussing programming, we will spend quite a lot of time discussing how to *get it right*: how to be sure that the computer program is calculating what you want it to calculate.

One distinguishing characteristic of statistical programming is that it is concerned with randomness: random errors in data, and models that include stochastic components. We will discuss methods for simulating random values with specified characteristics, and show how random simulations are useful in a variety of problems.

Many statistical procedures are based on linear models. While discussion of linear regression and other linear models is beyond the scope of this book, we do discuss some of the background linear algebra, and how the computations it involves can be carried out. We also discuss the general problem of numerical optimization: finding the values which make a function as large or as small as possible.

For instance string length in a tensegrity.

Each chapter has a number of exercises which are at varying degrees of difficulty. Solutions to selected exercises can be found on the web at www.stats.uwo.ca/faculty/braun/statprog. ← *Web site*

1.3 | The R package

This book uses R, which is an open-source package for statistical computing. "Open source" has a number of different meanings; here the important one is that R is freely available, and its users are free to see how it is written, and to improve it. R is based on the computer language S, developed by John Chambers and others at Bell Laboratories in 1976. In 1993 Robert Gentleman and Ross Ihaka at the University of Auckland wanted to experiment with the language, so they developed an implementation, and named it R. They made it open source in 1995, and hundreds of people around the world have contributed to its development.

S-PLUS is a commercial implementation of the S language. Because both R and S-PLUS are based on the S language, much of what is described in what follows will apply without change to S-PLUS.

1.4 | Why use a command line?

The R system is mainly command-driven, with the user typing in text and asking R to execute it. Nowadays most programs use interactive graphical user interfaces (menus, etc.) instead. So why did we choose such an old-fashioned way of doing things?

Menu-based interfaces are very convenient when applied to a limited set of commands, from a few to one or two hundred. However, a command-line interface is open ended. As we will show in this book, if you want to program a computer to do something that no one has done before, you can easily do it by breaking down the task into the parts that make it up, and then building up a program to carry it out. This may be possible in some menu-driven interfaces, but it is much easier in a command-driven interface.

Moreover, learning how to use one command line interface will give you skills that carry over to others, and may even give you some insight into how a menu-driven interface is implemented. As statisticians it is our belief that your goal should be understanding, and learning how to program at a command line will give you that at a fundamental level. Learning to use a } *Yes* menu-based program makes you dependent on the particular organization of that program.

There is a fairly rich menu-driven interface to R available in the Rcmdr package.[1] After you have worked through this book, if you come upon a statistical task that you don't know how to start, you may find that the menus in Rcmdr give you an idea of what methods are available.

[1] A package is a collection of functions and programs that can be used within R.

1.5 | Font conventions

This book describes how to do computations in R. As we will see in the next chapter, this requires that the user types input, and R responds with text or graphs as output. To indicate the difference, we have typeset the user input in a slanted typewriter font, and text output in an upright version of the same font. For example,

```
> This was typed by the user
This is a response from R
```

In most cases other than this one and certain exercises, we will show the actual response from R.[2]

There are also situations where the code is purely illustrative and is not meant to be executed. (Many of those are not correct R code at all; others illustrate the syntax of R code in a general way.) In these situations we have typeset the code examples in an upright typewriter font. For example,

```
f( some arguments )
```

1.6 | Installation of R

⌐ Web site

R can be downloaded from http://cran.r-project.org. Most users should download and install a *binary version*. This is a version that has been translated (by *compilers*) into machine language for execution on a particular type of computer with a particular operating system. R is designed to be very *portable*: it will run on Microsoft Windows, Linux, Solaris, Mac OSX, and other operating systems, but different binary versions are required for each. In this book most of what we do would be the same on any system, but when we write system-specific instructions, we will assume that readers are using Microsoft Windows.

Installation on Microsoft Windows is straightforward. A binary version is available for Windows 98 or above from the web page http://cran.r-project.org/bin/windows/base.
Download the "setup program," a file with a name like R-2.5.1-win32.exe. Clicking on this file will start an almost automatic installation of the R system. Though it is possible to customize the installation, the default responses will lead to a satisfactory installation in most situations, particularly for beginning users.

One of the default settings of the installation procedure is to create an R icon on your computer's desktop.

Once you have installed R, you will be ready to start statistical programming. Let's learn how.

[2] We have used the Sweave package so that R itself is computing the output. The computations in the text were done with a pre-release version of R 2.5.0.

2

Introduction to the R language

Having installed the R system, you are now ready to begin to learn the art of statistical programming. The first step is to learn the *syntax* of the language that you will be programming in; you need to know the rules of the language. This chapter will give you an introduction to the syntax of R.

2.1 | Starting and quitting R

In Microsoft Windows, the R installer will have created a Start Menu item and an icon for R on your desktop. Double clicking on the R icon starts the program.[1] The first thing that will happen is that R will open the *console*, into which the user can type commands.

The greater-than sign (>) is the prompt symbol. When this appears, you can begin typing commands.

For example, R can be used as a calculator. We can type simple arithmetical expressions at the > prompt:

```
> 5 + 49
```

Upon pressing the **Enter** key, the result 54 appears, prefixed by the number 1 in square brackets:

```
> 5 + 49
[1] 54
```

The [1] indicates that this is the first (and in this case only) result from the command. Other commands return multiple values, and each line of results will be labeled to aid the user in deciphering the output. For example, the sequence of integers from 1 to 20 may be displayed as follows:

```
> options(width=40)
> 1:20
 [1]  1  2  3  4  5  6  7  8  9 10 11 12
[13] 13 14 15 16 17 18 19 20
```

[1] Other systems may install an icon to click, or may require you to type "R" at a command prompt.

The first line starts with the first return value, so is labeled [1]; the second line starts with the 13th, so is labeled [13].[2]

Anything that can be computed on a pocket calculator can be computed at the R prompt. Here are some additional examples:

```
> #   "*" is the symbol for multiplication.
> # Everything following a # sign is assumed to be a
> # comment and is ignored by R.
> 3 * 5
[1] 15
> 3 - 8
[1] -5
> 12 / 4
[1] 3
```

To quit your R session, type

```
> q()
```

If you then hit the **Enter** key, you will be asked whether to save an image of the current workspace, or not, or to cancel. The workspace image contains a record of the computations you've done, and may contain some saved results. Hitting the **Cancel** option allows you to continue your current R session. We rarely save the current workspace image, but occasionally find it convenient to do so.

Note what happens if you omit the parentheses () when attempting to quit:

```
> q
function (save = "default", status = 0, runLast = TRUE)
.Internal(quit(save, status, runLast))
<environment: namespace:base>
```

This has happened because q is a *function* that is used to tell R to quit. Typing q by itself tells R to show us the (not very pleasant-looking) contents of the function q. By typing q(), we are telling R to *call* the function q. The action of this function is to quit R. *Everything* that R does is done through calls to functions, though sometimes those calls are hidden (as when we click on menus), or very basic (as when we call the multiplication function to multiply 3 times 5).

2.1.1   Recording your work

Rather than saving the workspace, we prefer to keep a record of the commands we entered, so that we can reproduce the workspace at a later date. In Windows, the easiest way to do this is to enter commands in R's script editor, available from the File menu. Commands are executed by highlighting them and hitting Ctrl-R (which stands for "run"). At the end of a session, save the final script for a permanent record of your work. In other systems a text editor and some form of cut and paste serve the same purpose.

[2] The position of the line break shown here depends on the optional setting options(width=40). Other choices of line widths would break in different places.

2.2 | Basic features of R

2.2.1 Calculating with R

At its most basic level, R can be viewed as a fancy calculator. We saw in the previous section that it can be used to do scalar arithmetic. The basic operations are + (add), − (subtract), * (multiply), and / (divide).

It can also be used to compute powers with the ^ operator. For example,

```
> 3^4
[1] 81
```

Modular arithmetic is also available. For example, we can compute the remainder after division of 31 by 7, i.e. 31 (mod 7):

```
> 31 %% 7
[1] 3
```

and the integer part of a fraction as

```
> 31 %/% 7
[1] 4
```

We can confirm that 31 is the sum of its remainder plus seven times the integer part of the fraction:

```
> 7 * 4 + 3
[1] 31
```

2.2.2 Named storage

R has a workspace known as the *global environment* that can be used to store the results of calculations, and many other types of objects. For a first example, suppose we would like to store the result of the calculation 1.0025^30 for future use. (This number arises out of a compound interest calculation based on an interest rate of 0.25% per year and a 30-year period.) We will assign this value to an object called interest.30. To this, we type

```
> interest.30 <- 1.0025^30
>
```

We tell R to make the assignment using an arrow that points to the left, created with the less-than sign (<) and the hyphen (−). R also supports using the equals sign (=) in place of the arrow in most circumstances, but we recommend using the arrow, as it makes clear that we are requesting an *action* (i.e. an assignment), rather than stating a *relation* (i.e. that interest.30 is equal to 1.0025^30) or making a permanent definition. Note that when we hit **Enter**, nothing appears on the screen except a new prompt: R has done what we asked, and is waiting for us to ask for something else.

We can see the results of this assignment by typing the name of our new object at the prompt:

```
> interest.30
[1] 1.077783
```

Think of this as just another calculation: R is calculating the result of the expression `interest.30`, and printing it. We can also use `interest.30` in further calculations if we wish. For example, we can calculate the bank balance after 30 years at 0.25% annual interest, if we start with an initial balance of $3000:

```
> initial.balance <- 3000
> final.balance <- initial.balance * interest.30
> final.balance
[1] 3233.35
```

Example 2.1

An individual wishes to take out a loan, today, of P at a monthly interest rate i. The loan is to be paid back in n monthly installments of size R, beginning one month from now. The problem is to calculate R.

Equating the present value P to the future (discounted) value of the n monthly payments R, we have

$$P = R(1+i)^{-1} + R(1+i)^{-2} + \cdots + R(1+i)^{-n}$$

or

$$P = R \sum_{j=1}^{n} (1+i)^{-j}.$$

Summing this geometric series and simplifying, we obtain

$$P = R \left(\frac{1 - (1+i)^{-n}}{i} \right).$$

This is the formula for the present value of an annuity. We can find R, given P, n and i as

$$R = P \frac{i}{1 - (1+i)^{-n}}.$$

In R, we define variables as follows: `principal` to hold the value of P, and `intRate` to hold the interest rate, and `n` to hold the number of payments. We will assign the resulting payment value to an object called `payment`.

Of course, we need some numerical values to work with, so we will suppose that the loan amount is $1500, the interest rate is 1% and the number of payments is 10. The required code is then

```
> intRate <- 0.01
> n <- 10
> principal <- 1500
> payment <- principal * intRate / (1 - (1 + intRate)^(-n))
```

```
> payment
[1] 158.3731
```

For this particular loan, the monthly payments are $158.37.

2.2.3 Functions

Most of the work in R is done through *functions*. For example, we saw that to quit R we type q(). This tells R to *call* the function named q. The parentheses surround the *argument list*, which in this case contains nothing: we just want R to quit, and do not need to tell it how.

We also saw that q is defined as

```
> q
function (save = "default", status = 0, runLast = TRUE)
.Internal(quit(save, status, runLast))
<environment: namespace:base>
```

This shows that q is a function that has three *arguments*: save, status, and runLast. Each of those has a *default value*: "default", 0, and TRUE, respectively. What happens when we execute q() is that R calls the q function with the arguments set to their default values.

If we want to change the default values, we specify them when we call the function. Arguments are identified in the call by their position, or by specifying the name explicitly. For example, both

```
q("no")
q(save = "no")
```

tell R to call q with the first argument set to "no", i.e. to quit without saving the workspace. If we had given two arguments without names, they would apply to save and status. If we want to accept the defaults of the early parameters but change later ones, we give the name when calling the function, e.g.

```
q(runLast = FALSE)
```

or use commas to mark the missing arguments, e.g.

```
q( , , FALSE)
```

It is a good idea to use named arguments when calling a function which has many arguments or when using uncommon arguments, because it reduces the risk of specifying the wrong argument, and makes your code easier to read.

2.2.4 Exact or approximate?

One important distinction in computing is between exact and approximate results. Most of what we do in this book is aimed at approximate methods. It is possible in a computer to represent any rational number exactly, but it is more common to use approximate representations: usually *floating point representations*. These are a binary (base-two) variation on scientific notation. For example, we might write a number to four significant digits in scientific notation as 6.926×10^{-4}. This representation of a number could represent any true value between $0.000\,692\,55$ and $0.000\,692\,65$. Standard floating point representations on computers are similar, except that a power of 2 would be used rather than a power of 10, and the fraction would be written in binary notation. The number above would be written as $1.011_2 \times 2^{-11}$ if four binary digit precision was used. The subscript 2 in the mantissa 1.011_2 indicates that this number is shown in base 2; that is, it represents $1 \times 2^0 + 0 \times 2^{-1} + 1 \times 2^{-2} + 1 \times 2^{-3}$, or 1.375 in decimal notation.

However, 6.926×10^{-4} and $1.011_2 \times 2^{-11}$ are not identical. Four binary digits give less precision than four decimal digits: a range of values from approximately $0.000\,641$ to $0.000\,702$ would all get the same representation to four binary digit precision. In fact, 6.926×10^{-4} *cannot* be represented exactly in binary notation in a finite number of digits. The problem is similar to trying to represent $1/3$ as a decimal: 0.3333 is a close approximation, but is not exact. The standard precision in R is 53 binary digits, which is equivalent to about 15 or 16 decimal digits.

To illustrate, consider the fractions $5/4$ and $4/5$. In decimal notation these can be represented exactly as 1.25 and 0.8 respectively. In binary notation $5/4$ is $1 + 1/4 = 1.01_2$. How do we determine the binary representation of $4/5$? It is between 0 and 1, so we'd expect something of the form $0.b_1 b_2 b_3 \cdots$, where each b_i represents a "bit," i.e. a 0 or 1 digit. Multiplying by 2 moves the all bits left by one, i.e. $2 \times 4/5 = 1.6 = b_1.b_2 b_3 \cdots$. Thus $b_1 = 1$, and $0.6 = 0.b_2 b_3 \cdots$.

We can now multiply by 2 again to find $2 \times 0.6 = 1.2 = b_2.b_3 \cdots$, so $b_2 = 1$. Repeating twice more yields $b_3 = b_4 = 0$. (Try it!)

At this point we'll have the number 0.8 again, so the sequence of 4 bits will repeat indefinitely: in base 2, $4/5$ is $0.110\,011\,001\,100\cdots$. Since R only stores 53 bits, it won't be able to store 0.8 exactly. Some rounding error will occur in the storage.

We can observe the rounding error with the following experiment. With exact arithmetic, $(5/4) \times (4/5) = 1$, so $(5/4) \times (n \times 4/5)$ should be exactly n for any value of n. But if we try this calculation in R, we find

```
> n <- 1:10
> 1.25 * (n * 0.8) - n
```

```
[1] 0.000000e+00 0.000000e+00 4.440892e-16 0.000000e+00 0.000000e+00
[6] 8.881784e-16 8.881784e-16 0.000000e+00 0.000000e+00 0.000000e+00
```

i.e. it is equal for some values, but not equal for $n = 3, 6$, or 7. The errors are very small, but nonzero.

Rounding error tends to accumulate in most calculations, so usually a long series of calculations will result in larger errors than a short one. Some operations are particularly prone to rounding error: for example, subtraction of two nearly equal numbers, or (equivalently) addition of two numbers with nearly the same magnitude but opposite signs. Since the leading bits in the binary expansions of nearly equal numbers will match, they will cancel in subtraction, and the result will depend on what is stored in the later bits.

Example 2.2
Consider the standard formula for the sample variance of a sample $x_1, \ldots, x_n$:

$$s^2 = \frac{1}{n-1} \sum_{i=1}^{n} (x_i - \bar{x})^2,$$

where $\bar{x}$ is the sample mean, $(1/n) \sum x_i$. In R, s^2 is available as `var()`, and $\bar{x}$ is `mean()`. For example:

```
> x <- 1:11
> mean(x)
[1] 6
> var(x)
[1] 11
> sum( (x - mean(x))^2 ) / 10
[1] 11
```

Because this formula requires calculation of $\bar{x}$ first and the sum of squared deviations second, it requires that all x_i values be kept in memory. Not too long ago memory was so expensive that it was advantageous to rewrite the formula as

$$s^2 = \frac{1}{n-1} \left(\sum_{i=1}^{n} x_i^2 - n\bar{x}^2 \right).$$

This is called the "one-pass formula," because we evaluate each x_i value just once, and accumulate the sums of x_i and of x_i^2. It gives the correct answer, both mathematically and in our example:

```
> ( sum(x^2) - 11 * mean(x)^2 ) / 10
[1] 11
```

However, notice what happens if we add a large value A to each x_i. The sum $\sum_{i=1}^{n} x_i^2$ increases by approximately nA^2, and so does $n\bar{x}^2$. This doesn't change the variance, but it provides the conditions for a "catastrophic loss of precision" when we take the difference:

```
> A <- 1.e10
> x <- 1:11 + A
> var(x)
[1] 11
> ( sum(x^2) - 11 * mean(x)^2 ) / 10
[1] 0
```

Since R gets the right answer, it clearly doesn't use the one-pass formula, and neither should you.

2.2.5 R is case-sensitive

See what happens if you type

```
> x <- 1:10
> MEAN(x)
Error: could not find function "MEAN"
```

or

```
> mean(x)
[1] 5.5
```

Now try

```
> MEAN <- mean
> MEAN(x)
[1] 5.5
```

The function mean() is built in to R. R considers MEAN to be a different function, because it is case-sensitive: m is a different letter than M.

2.2.6 Listing the objects in the workspace

The calculations in the previous sections led to the creation of several simple R objects. These objects are stored in the current R workspace. A list of all objects in the current workspace can be printed to the screen using the objects() function:

```
> objects()
 [1] "A"             "final.balance"   "initial.balance"
 [4] "interest.30"   "intRate"         "MEAN"
 [7] "n"             "payment"         "principal"
[10] "saveopt"       "x"
```

A synonym for objects() is ls().

Remember that if we quit our R session without saving the workspace image, then these objects will disappear. If we save the workspace image, then the workspace will be restored at our next R session.[3]

2.2.7 Vectors

A numeric vector is a list of numbers. The c() function is used to collect things together into a vector. We can type

```
> c(0, 7, 8)
[1] 0 7 8
```

Again, we can assign this to a named object:

```
> x <- c(0, 7, 8)   # now x is a 3-element vector
```

To see the contents of x, simply type

```
> x
[1] 0 7 8
```

[3] This will always be true if we start R from the same folder, or working directory, as where we ended the previous R session. Normally this will be the case, but users are free to change the folder during a session using the menus or the setwd() function.

The : symbol can be used to create sequences of increasing (or decreasing) values. For example,

```
> numbers5to20 <- 5:20
> numbers5to20
 [1]  5  6  7  8  9 10 11 12 13 14 15 16 17 18 19 20
```

Vectors can be joined together (i.e. *concatenated*) with the c function. For example, note what happens when we type

```
> c(numbers5to20, x)
 [1]  5  6  7  8  9 10 11 12 13 14 15 16 17 18 19 20  0  7  8
```

Here is another example of the use of the c() function:

```
> some.numbers <- c(2, 3, 5, 7, 11, 13, 17, 19, 23, 29, 31, 37, 41,
+    43, 47, 59, 67, 71, 73, 79, 83, 89, 97, 103, 107, 109, 113, 119)
```

Notice that R has prompted us with the + sign for a second line of input; it does this when the first line is incomplete.

We can append numbers5to20 to the end of some.numbers, and then append the decreasing sequence from 4 to 1:

```
> a.mess <- c(some.numbers, numbers5to20, 4:1)
> a.mess
 [1]   2   3   5   7  11  13  17  19  23  29  31  37  41  43  47  59
[17]  67  71  73  79  83  89  97 103 107 109 113 119   5   6   7   8
[33]   9  10  11  12  13  14  15  16  17  18  19  20   4   3   2   1
```

Remember that the numbers in the square brackets give the index of the element immediately to the right. Among other things, this helps us to identify the 22nd element of a.mess as 89.

2.2.8 Extracting elements from vectors

A nicer way to display the 22nd element of a.mess is to use square brackets to extract just that element:

```
> a.mess[22]
[1] 89
```

To print the second element of x, type

```
> x[2]
[1] 7
```

We can extract more than one element at a time. For example,

```
> some.numbers[c(3, 6, 7)]
[1]  5 13 17
```

To get the third through seventh elements of numbers5to20, type

```
> numbers5to20[3:7]
[1]  7  8  9 10 11
```

Negative indices can be used to avoid certain elements. For example, we can select all but the second element of x as follows:

```
> x[-2]
[1] 0 8
```

The third through eleventh elements of some.numbers can be avoided as follows:

```
> some.numbers[-(3:11)]
 [1]   2   3  37  41  43  47  59  67  71  73  79  83  89  97 103 107
[17] 109 113 119
```

Using a zero index returns nothing. This is not something that one would usually type, but it may be useful in more complicated expressions.

```
> numbers5to20[c(0, 3:7)]
[1]  7  8  9 10 11
```

Do not mix positive and negative indices. To see what happens, consider

```
> x[c(-2, 3)]
Error: only 0's may be mixed with negative subscripts
```

The problem is that it is not clear what is to be extracted: do we want the third element of x before or after removing the second one?

2.2.9 Vector arithmetic

Arithmetic can be done on R vectors. For example, we can multiply all elements of x by 3:

```
> x * 3
[1]  0 21 24
```

Note that the computation is performed elementwise. Addition, subtraction and division by a constant have the same kind of effect. For example,

```
> y <- x - 5
> y
[1] -5  2  3
```

For another example, consider taking the third power of the elements of x:

```
> x^3
[1]   0 343 512
```

The above examples show how a binary arithmetic operator can be used with vectors and constants. In general, the binary operators also work element-by-element when applied to pairs of vectors. For example, we can compute $y_i^{x_i}$, for $i = 1, 2, 3$, i.e. $(y_1^{x_1}, y_2^{x_2}, y_3^{x_3})$, as follows:

```
> y^x
[1]    1  128 6561
```

When the vectors are different lengths, the shorter one is extended by *recycling*: values are repeated, starting at the beginning. For example, to see the pattern of remainders of the numbers 1 to 10 modulo 2 and 3, we need only give the 2 : 3 vector once:

```
> c(1, 1, 2, 2, 3, 3, 4, 4, 5, 5,
+    6, 6, 7, 7, 8, 8, 9, 9, 10, 10) %% 2:3
[1] 1 1 0 2 1 0 0 1 1 2 0 0 1 1 0 2 1 0 0 1
```

R will give a warning if the length of the longer vector is not a multiple of the length of the smaller one, because that is usually a sign that something is wrong. For example, if we wanted the remainders modulo 2, 3, and 4, this is the wrong way to do it:

```
> c(1, 1, 2, 2, 3, 3, 4, 4, 5, 5,
+    6, 6, 7, 7, 8, 8, 9, 9, 10, 10) %% 2:4
[1] 1 1 2 0 0 3 0 1 1 1 0 2 1 1 0 0 0 1 0 1
Warning message:
longer object length
        is not a multiple of shorter object length in: c(1, 1, 2, 2,
        3, 3, 4, 4, 5, 5, 6, 6, 7, 7, 8, 8, 9, 9, 10, 10)%%2:4
```

(Do you see the error?)

2.2.10 Simple patterned vectors

We saw the use of the : operator for producing simple sequences of integers. Patterned vectors can also be produced using the seq() function as well as the rep() function. For example, the sequence of odd numbers less than or equal to 21 can be obtained using

```
seq(1, 21, by=2)
```

Notice the use of by=2 here. The seq() function has several *optional parameters*, including one named by. If by is not specified, the default value of 1 will be used.

Repeated patterns are obtained using rep(). Consider the following examples:

```
> rep(3, 12)          # repeat the value 3, 12 times
[1] 3 3 3 3 3 3 3 3 3 3 3 3
> rep(seq(2, 20, by=2), 2)     # repeat the pattern 2 4 ... 20, twice
[1]  2  4  6  8 10 12 14 16 18 20  2  4  6  8 10 12 14 16 18 20
> rep(c(1, 4), c(3, 2))   # repeat 1, 3 times and  4, twice
[1] 1 1 1 4 4
> rep(c(1, 4), each=3)    # repeat each value 3 times
[1] 1 1 1 4 4 4
> rep(seq(2, 20, 2), rep(2, 10))    # repeat each value twice
[1]  2  2  4  4  6  6  8  8 10 10 12 12 14 14 16 16 18 18 20 20
```

2.2.11   Missing values and other special values

The missing value symbol is NA. Missing values often arise in real data
problems, but they can also arise because of the way calculations are
performed.

```
> some.evens <- NULL        # creates a vector with no elements
> some.evens[seq(2, 20, 2)] <- seq(2, 20, 2)
> some.evens
 [1]  NA   2  NA   4  NA   6  NA   8  NA  10  NA  12  NA  14  NA  16  NA  18  NA  20
```

What happened here is that we assigned values to elements $2, 4, \ldots, 20$ but
never assigned anything to elements $1, 3, \ldots, 19$, so R uses NA to signal
that the value is unknown.

Recall that x contains the values $(0, 7, 8)$. Consider

```
> x / x
[1] NaN   1   1
```

The NaN symbol denotes a value which is "not a number," which arises
as a result of attempting to compute the indeterminate $0/0$. This symbol is sometimes used when a calculation does not make sense. In other
cases, special values may be shown, or you may get an error or warning
message:

```
> 1 / x
[1]       Inf 0.1428571 0.1250000
```

Here, R has tried to evaluate $1/0$.

Always be careful to make sure that vector indices are integers. When
fractional values are used, they will be truncated towards 0. Thus 0.4
becomes 0, and we see

```
> x[0.4]
numeric(0)
```

The output numeric(0) indicates a numeric vector of length zero.

2.2.12   Character vectors

Scalars and vectors can be made up of strings of characters instead of
numbers. All elements of a vector must be of the same type. For example,

```
> colors <- c("red", "yellow", "blue")
> more.colors <- c(colors, "green", "magenta", "cyan")
>                              # this appended some new elements to colors
> z <- c("red", "green", 1)  # an attempt to mix data types in a vector
```

To see the contents of more.colors and z, simply type

```
> more.colors
[1] "red"      "yellow"  "blue"      "green"    "magenta" "cyan"
> z                            # 1 has been converted to the character "1"
[1] "red"      "green" "1"
```

There are two basic operations you might want to perform on character vectors. To take substrings, use `substr()`. The former takes arguments `substr(x, start, stop)`, where `x` is a vector of character strings, and `start` and `stop` say which characters to keep. For example, to print the first two letters of each color use

```
> substr(colors, 1, 2)
[1] "re" "ye" "bl"
```

The `substring()` function is similar, but with slightly different definitions of the arguments: see the help page `?substring`.

The other basic operation is building up strings by concatenation. Use the `paste()` function for this. For example,

```
> paste(colors, "flowers")
[1] "red flowers"    "yellow flowers" "blue flowers"
```

There are two optional parameters to `paste()`. The `sep` parameter controls what goes between the components being pasted together. We might not want the default space, for example:

```
> paste("several ", colors, "s", sep="")
[1] "several reds"    "several yellows" "several blues"
```

The `collapse` parameter to `paste()` allows all the components of the resulting vector to be collapsed into a single string:

```
> paste("I like", colors, collapse = ", ")
[1] "I like red, I like yellow, I like blue"
```

2.2.13   Factors

Factors offer an alternative way of storing character data. For example, a factor with four elements and having the two levels, `control` and `treatment` can be created using:

```
> grp <- c("control", "treatment", "control", "treatment")
> grp
[1] "control"   "treatment" "control"   "treatment"
> grp <- factor(grp)
> grp
[1] control   treatment control   treatment
Levels: control treatment
```

Factors are a more efficient way of storing character data when there are repeats among the vector elements. This is because the levels of a factor are internally coded as integers. To see what the codes are for our factor, we can type

```
> as.integer(grp)
[1] 1 2 1 2
```

The labels for the levels are only stored once each, rather than being repeated. The codes are indices into the vector of levels:

```
> levels(grp)
[1] "control"    "treatment"
> levels(grp)[as.integer(grp)]
[1] "control"    "treatment" "control"    "treatment"
```

2.2.14 More on extracting elements from vectors

As for numeric vectors, square brackets [] are used to index factor and character vector elements. For example, the factor grp has four elements, so we can print out the third element by typing

```
> grp[3]
[1] control
Levels: control treatment
```

We can access the second through fifth elements of more.colors as follows:

```
> more.colors[2:5]
[1] "yellow"   "blue"      "green"      "magenta"
```

When there may be missing values, the is.na() function should be used to detect them. For instance,

```
> is.na(some.evens)
 [1]   TRUE FALSE   TRUE FALSE   TRUE FALSE   TRUE FALSE   TRUE FALSE   TRUE
[12] FALSE   TRUE FALSE   TRUE FALSE   TRUE FALSE   TRUE FALSE
```

(The result is a "logical vector". More on these in Section 2.4 below.) The ! symbol means "not", so we can locate the non-missing values in some.evens as follows:

```
> !is.na(some.evens)
 [1] FALSE   TRUE FALSE   TRUE FALSE   TRUE FALSE   TRUE FALSE   TRUE FALSE
[12]   TRUE FALSE   TRUE FALSE   TRUE FALSE   TRUE FALSE   TRUE
```

We can then display the even numbers only:

```
> some.evens[!is.na(some.evens)]
 [1]   2   4   6   8  10  12  14  16  18  20
```

2.2.15 Matrices and arrays

To arrange values into a matrix, we use the matrix() function:

```
> m <- matrix(1:6, nrow=2, ncol=3)
> m
     [,1] [,2] [,3]
[1,]    1    3    5
[2,]    2    4    6
```

We can then access elements using two indices. For example, the value in the first row, second column is

```
> m[1, 2]
[1] 3
```

Somewhat confusingly, R also allows a matrix to be indexed as a vector, using just one value:

```
> m[4]
[1] 4
```

Here elements are selected in the order in which they are stored internally: down the first column, then down the second, and so on. This is known as *column-major* storage order. Some computer languages use *row-major* storage order, where values are stored in order from left to right across the first row, then left to right across the second, and so on.

Whole rows or columns of matrices may be selected by leaving the corresponding index blank:

```
> m[1,]
[1] 1 3 5
> m[, 1]
[1] 1 2
```

A more general way to store data is in an *array*. Arrays have multiple indices, and are created using the array function:

```
> a <- array(1:24, c(3, 4, 2))
> a
, , 1
     [,1] [,2] [,3] [,4]
[1,]    1    4    7   10
[2,]    2    5    8   11
[3,]    3    6    9   12
, , 2
     [,1] [,2] [,3] [,4]
[1,]   13   16   19   22
[2,]   14   17   20   23
[3,]   15   18   21   24
```

Notice that the dimensions were specified in a vector c(3, 4, 2). When inserting data, the first index varies fastest; when it has run through its full range, the second index changes, etc.

2.2.16 Data frames

Most data sets are stored in R as data frames. These are like matrices, but with the columns having their own names. Columns can be of different types from each other. Use the data.frame() function to construct data frames from vectors:

```
> colors <- c("red", "yellow", "blue")
> numbers <- c(1, 2, 3)
> colors.and.numbers <- data.frame(colors, numbers,
+                                  more.numbers=c(4, 5, 6))
```

We can see the contents of a data frame:

```
> colors.and.numbers
  colors numbers more.numbers
1    red       1            4
2 yellow       2            5
3   blue       3            6
```

Exercises

1 Calculate the remainder after dividing 31 079 into 170 166 719.

2 Calculate the monthly payment required for a loan of $200 000, at a monthly interest rate of 0.003, based on 300 monthly payments, starting in one month's time.

3 Calculate the sum $\sum_{j=1}^{n} r^j$, where r has been assigned the value 1.08, and compare with $(1 - r^{n+1})/(1 - r)$, for $n = 10, 20, 30, 40$. Repeat for $r = 1.06$.

4 Referring to the above question, use the quick formula to compute $\sum_{j=1}^{n} r^j$, for $r = 1.08$, for all values of n between 1 and 100. Store the 100 values in a vector.

5 Calculate the sum $\sum_{j=1}^{n} j$ and compare with $n(n + 1)/2$, for $n = 100, 200, 400, 800$.

6 Referring to the above question, use the quick formula to compute $\sum_{j=1}^{n} j$ for all values of n between 1 and 100. Store the 100 values in a vector.

7 Calculate the sum $\sum_{j=1}^{n} j^2$ and compare with $n(n + 1)(2n + 1)/6$, for $n = 200, 400, 600, 800$.

8 Referring to the above question, use the quick formula to compute $\sum_{j=1}^{n} j^2$ for all values of n between 1 and 100. Store the 100 values in a vector.

9 Calculate the sum $\sum_{i=1}^{N} 1/i$, and compare with $\log(N) + 0.6$, for $N = 500, 1000, 2000, 4000, 8000$.

10 Can you explain these two results? (Hint: see Section 2.2.4.)

```
> x <- c(0,7,8)
> x[0.9999999999999999]
numeric(0)
> x[0.99999999999999999]
[1] 0
```

11 Using rep() and seq() as needed, create the vectors

```
0 0 0 0 0 1 1 1 1 1 2 2 2 2 2 3 3 3 3 3 4 4 4 4 4
```

and

```
1 2 3 4 5 1 2 3 4 5 1 2 3 4 5 1 2 3 4 5 1 2 3 4 5
```

12 Using `rep()` and `seq()` as needed, create the vector

```
1 2 3 4 5 2 3 4 5 6 3 4 5 6 7 4 5 6 7 8 5 6 7 8 9
```

13 Use the `more.colors` vector, `rep()` and `seq()` to create the vector

```
"red"     "yellow"  "blue"     "yellow"  "blue"     "green"
"blue"    "green"   "magenta"  "green"   "magenta"  "cyan"
```

2.2.17 Dates and times

Dates and times are among the most difficult types of data to work with on computers. The standard calendar is very complicated: months of different lengths, leap years every four years (with exceptions for whole centuries) and so on. When looking at dates over historical time periods, changes to the calendar (such as the switch from the Julian calendar to the modern Gregorian calendar that occurred in various countries between 1582 and 1923) affect the interpretation of dates.

Times are also messy, because there is often an unstated time zone (which may change for some dates due to daylight savings time), and some years have "leap seconds" added in order to keep standard clocks consistent with the rotation of the earth.

There have been several attempts to deal with this in R. The base package has the function `strptime()` to convert from strings (e.g. `"2007-12-25"`, or `"12/25/07"`) to an internal numerical representation, and `format()` to convert back for printing. The `ISOdate()` and `ISOdatetime()` functions are used when numerical values for the year, month day, etc. are known. Other functions are available in the `chron` package. These can be difficult functions to use, and a full description is beyond the scope of this book.

2.3 | Built-in functions and online help

The function `q()` is an example of a built-in function. There are many functions in R which are designed to do all sorts of things. The online help facility can help you to see what a particular function is supposed to do. There are a number of ways of accessing the help facility.

If you know the name of the function that you need help with, the `help()` function is likely sufficient. For example, for help on the `q()` function, type

```
> ?q
```

or

```
> help(q)
```

Either of these commands opens a window which will give you a description of the function for quitting R.

Another commonly used function in R is mean(). Upon typing

```
> help(mean)
```

a new window will appear. The first part of its contents is

```
mean                    package:base                    R Documentation

Arithmetic Mean

Description:

     Generic function for the (trimmed) arithmetic mean.

Usage:

     mean(x, ...)

     ## Default S3 method:
     mean(x, trim = 0, na.rm = FALSE, ...)

  Arguments:

       x: An R object.  Currently there are methods for numeric data
          frames, numeric vectors and dates.  A complex vector is
          allowed for 'trim = 0', only.

    trim: the fraction (0 to 0.5) of observations to be trimmed from
          each end of 'x' before the mean is computed.
```

(There may be small differences in the display on your system.) This tells us that mean() will compute the ordinary arithmetic average or it will do something called "trimming" if we ask for it.

To compute the mean of the values of the x vector created earlier, we simply type

```
> mean(x)
[1] 5
```

2.3.1 Built-in examples

A useful alternative to help() is the example() function:

```
> example(mean)
mean> x <- c(0:10, 50)

mean> xm <- mean(x)

mean> c(xm, mean(x, trim = 0.10))
[1] 8.75 5.50

mean> mean(USArrests, trim = 0.2)
  Murder   Assault  UrbanPop     Rape
    7.42    167.60     66.20    20.16
```

This example shows simple use of the mean() function as well as how to use the trim argument. (When trim=0.1, the highest 10% and lowest 10% of the data are deleted before the average is calculated.)

2.3.2 Finding help when you don't know the function name

It is often convenient to use help.start(). This brings up an Internet browser, such as Internet Explorer or Firefox.[4] The browser will show you a menu of several options, including a listing of installed packages. The base package contains many of the routinely used functions.

Another function that is often used is help.search(). For example, to see if there are any functions that do optimization (finding minima or maxima), type

```
help.search("optimization")
```

Here is the result of a such a search:

```
Help files with alias or concept or title matching "optimization" using
fuzzy matching:

lmeScale(nlme)            Scale for lme Optimization
optimization(OPM)         minimize linear function with linear
                          constraints
constrOptim(stats)        Linearly constrained optimisation
nlm(stats)                Non-Linear Minimization
optim(stats)              General-purpose Optimization

optimize(stats)           One Dimensional Optimization
portfolio.optim(tseries)
                          Portfolio Optimization

Type "help(FOO, package = PKG)" to inspect entry "FOO(PKG) TITLE".
```

We can then check for specific help on a function like nlm() by typing

```
help(nlm)
```

Web search engines such as Google can be useful for finding help on R. Including "R" as a keyword in such a search will often bring up the relevant R help page.[5] The name of the R package that is needed is usually listed at the top of the help page.

Another function to note is RSiteSearch() which will do a search in the R-help mailing list and other web resources. For example, to bring up information on the treatment of missing values in R, we can type

```
RSiteSearch("missing")
```

2.3.3 Built-in graphics functions

Two basic plots are the histogram and the scatterplot. Consider

```
> x <- c(12, 15, 13, 20, 14, 16, 10, 10, 8, 15)
> hist(x)
```

[4] R depends on your system having a properly installed browser. If it doesn't have one, you may see an error message, or possibly nothing at all.

[5] You may find pages describing functions that you do not have installed, because they are in user-contributed packages.

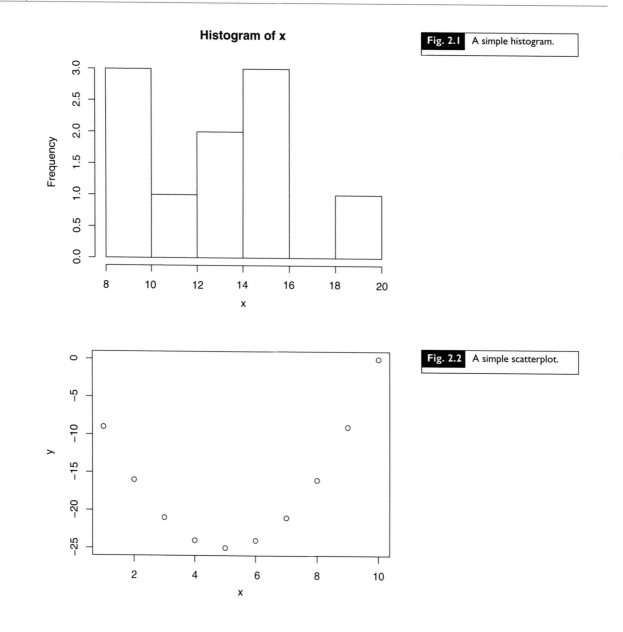

Histogram of x

Fig. 2.1 A simple histogram.

Fig. 2.2 A simple scatterplot.

(see Figure 2.1) and

```
> x <- seq(1, 10)
> y <- x^2 - 10 * x
> plot(x, y)
```

(see Figure 2.2). Note that the x values are plotted along the horizontal axis.

Another useful plotting function is the `curve()` function for plotting the graph of a univariate mathematical function on an interval. The left and right endpoints of the interval are specified by `from` and `to` arguments, respectively.

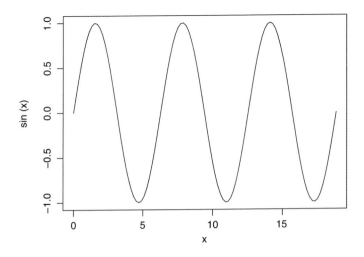

Fig. 2.3 Plotting the sin curve.

A simple example involves plotting the sine function on the interval $[0, 6\pi]$:

```
> curve(expr = sin, from = 0, to = 6 * pi)
```

(see Figure 2.3). The `expr` parameter is either a function (whose output is a numeric vector when the input is a numeric vector) or an expression in terms of x. An example of the latter type of usage is:

```
curve(x^2 - 10 * x, from = 1, to = 10)
```

More information on graphics can be found in Chapter 3.

2.3.4 Additional elementary built-in functions

The sample median

The sample median measures the middle value of a data set. If the data are $x[1] \leq x[2] \leq \cdots \leq x[n]$, then the median is $x[(n + 1)/2]$, if n is odd, or $\{[x[n/2] + x[n/2 + 1]\}/2$, if n is even.

For example, the median of the values: $10, 10, 18, 30, 32$ is 18, and the median of $40, 10, 10, 18, 30, 32$ is the average of 18 and 30, i.e. 24.

This calculation is handled by R as follows:

```
median(x)   # computes the median or 50th percentile of the data in x
```

Other summary measures

Summary statistics can be calculated for data stored in vectors. In particular, try

```
var(x)      # computes the variance of the data in x
summary(x)  # computes several summary statistics on the data in x
```

Exercises

1 The following are a sample of observations on incoming solar radiation at a greenhouse:

```
11.1 10.6 6.3  8.8  10.7 11.2 8.9 12.2
```

(a) Assign the data to an object called `solar.radiation`.

(b) Find the mean, median and variance of the radiation observations.

(c) Add 10 to each observation of `solar.radiation`, and assign the result to `sr10`. Find the mean, median, and variance of `sr10`. Which statistics change, and by how much?

(d) Multiply each observation by −2, and assign the result to `srm2`. Find the mean, median, and variance of `srm2`. How do the statistics change now?

(e) Plot a histogram of the `solar.radiation`, `sr10`, and `srm2`.

(f) There are two formulas commonly used for the variance of a set of numbers: $(1/n) \sum_{i=1}^{n} (x_i - \bar{x})^2$ and $[1/(n-1)] \sum_{i=1}^{n} (x_i - \bar{x})^2$. One uses the sample size n in the denominator, and the other uses $n - 1$. Which formula does the `var()` function in R use?

2.4 | Logical vectors and relational operators

We have used the `c()` function to put numeric vectors together as well as character vectors. R also supports logical vectors. These contain two different elements: `TRUE` and `FALSE`.

2.4.1 Boolean algebra

To understand how R handles `TRUE` and `FALSE`, we need to understand a little "Boolean algebra." The idea of Boolean algebra is to formalize a mathematical approach to logic.

Logic deals with statements that are either true or false. We represent each statement by a letter or variable, e.g. A is the statement that the sky is clear, and B is the statement that it is raining. Depending on the weather where you are, those two statements may both be true (there is a "sunshower"), A may be true and B false (the usual clear day), A false and B true (the usual rainy day), or both may be false (a cloudy but dry day).

Boolean algebra tells us how to evaluate the truth of compound statements. For example, "A and B" is the statement that it is both clear and raining. This statement is only true during a sunshower. "A or B" says that it is clear or it is raining, or both: anything but the cloudy dry day. This is sometimes called an *inclusive or*, to distinguish it from the *exclusive or* "A xor B," which says that it is either clear or raining, but *not* both. There is also the "not A" statement, which says that it is not clear.

There is a very important relation between Boolean algebra and set theory. If we interpret A and B as sets, then we can think of "A and B" as the set of elements which are in A and are in B, i.e. the intersection $A \cap B$. Similarly "A or B" can be interpreted as the set of elements that are in A or are in B, i.e. the union $A \cup B$. Finally, "not A" is the complement of A, i.e. A^c.

Because there are only two possible values (true and false), we can record all Boolean operations in a table. On the first line of Table 2.1 we list the basic Boolean expressions, on the second line the equivalent way to code them in R, and in the body of the table the results of the operations.

Table 2.1.	*Truth table for Boolean operations*					
Boolean	*A*	*B*	not *A*	not *B*	*A* and *B*	*A* or *B*
R	A	B	!A	!B	A & B	A | B
	TRUE	TRUE	FALSE	FALSE	TRUE	TRUE
	TRUE	FALSE	FALSE	TRUE	FALSE	TRUE
	FALSE	TRUE	TRUE	FALSE	FALSE	TRUE
	FALSE	FALSE	TRUE	TRUE	FALSE	FALSE

Exercises

1 More complicated expressions can be constructed from the basic Boolean operations. Write out the truth table for the *xor* operator, and show how to write it in terms of *and*, *or*, and *not*.

2 Venn diagrams can be used to illustrate set unions and intersections. Draw Venn diagrams that correspond to the *and*, *or*, *not*, and *xor* operations.

3 DeMorgan's laws in R notation are !(A & B) == (!A) | (!B) and !(A | B) == (!A) & (!B). Write these out in English using the *A* and *B* statements above, and use truth tables to confirm each equality.

2.4.2 Logical operations in R

One of the basic types of vector in R holds logical values. For example, a logical vector may be constructed as

```
> a <- c(TRUE, FALSE, FALSE, TRUE)
```

The result is a vector of four logical values. Logical vectors may be used as indices:

```
> b <- c(13, 7, 8, 2)
> b[a]
[1] 13  2
```

The elements of b corresponding to TRUE are selected.

If we attempt arithmetic on a logical vector, e.g.

```
> sum(a)
[1] 2
```

then the operations are performed after converting FALSE to 0 and TRUE to 1. In this case the result is that we count how many occurrences of TRUE are in the vector.

There are two versions of the Boolean operators. The usual versions are &, |, and !, as listed in the previous section. These are all vectorized, so we see for example

```
> !a
[1] FALSE  TRUE  TRUE FALSE
```

If we attempt logical operations on a numerical vector, 0 is taken to be FALSE, and any nonzero value is taken to be TRUE:

```
> a & (b - 2)
[1]   TRUE FALSE FALSE FALSE
```

The operators && and || are similar to & and |, but behave differently in two respects. First, they are *not* vectorized: only one calculation is done. Secondly, they are guaranteed to be evaluated from left to right, with the right-hand operand only evaluated if necessary. For example, if A is FALSE, then A && B will be FALSE regardless of the value of B, so B needn't be evaluated. This can save time if evaluating B would be very slow, and may make calculations easier, for example if evaluating B would cause an error when A was FALSE. This behavior is sometimes called *short-circuit evaluation*.

Exercises

1 Under what circumstances would B need to be evaluated in the expression A || B?

2 Using the values from the previous section, predict the output from each of these expressions, and then try them in R.

```
min(b)
min(a)
max(b)
max(a)
length(a)
```

3 Type

```
b * a
```

2.4.3   Relational operators

It is often necessary to test relations when programming to decide whether they are TRUE or FALSE. R allows for equality and inequality relations to be tested in using the relational operators: <, >, ==, >=, <=, !=.

Examples:

• Type

```
a <- c(3, 6, 9)
```

• To test which elements are greater than 4, type

```
a > 4
```

• To test which elements are exactly equal[6] to 4, type

```
a == 4
```

• To test which elements are greater than or equal to 4, type

```
a >= 4
```

[6] Be careful with tests of equality. Because R works with only a limited number of decimal places rounding error can accumulate, and you may find surprising results, such as *49 * (4/49)* not being equal to *4*.

- To test which elements are not equal to 4, type

```
a != 4
```

- To print the elements of a which are greater than 4, type

```
a[a > 4]
```

- Type

```
b <- c(4, 6, 8)
```

- To test which elements of a are less than the corresponding elements of b, type

```
a < b
```

- To print the elements of a that are less than the corresponding elements of b, type

```
a[a < b]
```

2.5 | Data input and output

When in an R session, it is possible to read and write data to files outside of R, for example on your computer's hard drive. Before we can discuss some of the many ways of doing this, it is important to know where the data is coming from or going to.

2.5.1 Changing directories

In Windows versions of R, it is possible to use the **File | Change dir...** menu to choose the directory or folder to which you wish to direct your data.

It is also possible to use the `setwd()` function. For example, to work with data in the folder **mydata** on the **C:** drive, type

```
setwd("c:/mydata")     # or setwd("c:\\ mydata")
```

From now on, all data input and output will default to the **mydata** folder in the **C:** drive.[7]

2.5.2 dump() and source()

Suppose you have constructed an R object called `usefuldata`. In order to save this object for a future session, type

```
dump("usefuldata", "useful.R")
```

This stores the command necessary to create the vector `usefuldata` into the file *useful.R* on your computer's hard drive. The choice of filename is up to you, as long as it conforms to the usual requirements for filenames on your computer.

[7] If you are used to folder names in Windows, you might have expected this to be written as `"c:\mydata"`. However, R treats the backslash character "\" as a special "escape" character, which modifies the interpretation of the next character. If you really want a backslash, you need to double it: the first backslash tells the second backslash not to be an escape. Because other systems use a forward slash "/" in their folder names, and because doubling the backslash is tedious in Windows, R accepts either form.

To retrieve the vector in a future session, type

```
source("useful.R")
```

This reads and executes the command in *useful.R*, resulting in the creation of the `usefuldata` object in your global environment. If there was an object of the same name there before, it will be replaced.

To save all of the objects that you have created during a session, type

```
dump(list=objects(), "all.R")
```

This produces a file called *all.R* on your computer's hard drive. Using `source("all.R")` at a later time will allow you to retrieve all of these objects.

To save existing objects `humidity`, `temp` and `rain` to a file called *weather.R* on your hard drive, type

```
dump(c("humidity", "temp", "rain"), "weather.R")
```

Exercises

1 Use a text editor to create a file consisting of the line

```
randomdata <- c(64, 38, 97, 88, 24, 14, 104, 83)
```

Save it to a file called `randomdata`.

2 Source the file `randomdata` into R and confirm the `randomdata` vector was created.

3 Create a vector called `numbers` which contains

```
3 5 8 10 12
```

Dump `numbers` to a file called *numbers.R* and delete `numbers` using the `rm()` function. Using `ls()`, confirm that `numbers` has been deleted. Now, use the source command to retrieve the vector `numbers`.

2.5.3 Redirecting R output

By default, R directs the output of most of its functions to the screen. Output can be directed to a file with the `sink()` function.

As an example, consider the greenhouse data in the vector `solar.radiation`. The command `mean(solar.radiation)` prints the mean of the data to the screen. To print this to a file called *solarmean.txt*, type

```
sink("solarmean.txt")    # Create a file solarmean.txt for output
mean(solar.radiation)    # Write mean value to solarmean.txt
```

All subsequent output will be printed to the file *solarmean.txt* until the command

```
sink()                   # Close solarmean.txt; print new output to screen
```

is invoked. This returns subsequent output to the screen.

2.5.4 Saving and retrieving image files

The vectors and other objects created during an R session are stored in the workspace known as the global environment. When ending an R session, we have the option of saving the workspace in a file called a workspace image. If we choose to do so, a file called by default *.RData* is created in the current working directory (folder) which contains the information needed to reconstruct this workspace. In Windows, the workspace image will be automatically loaded if R is started by clicking on the icon representing the file *.RData*, or if the *.RData* file is saved in the directory from which R is started. If R is started in another directory, the `load()` function may be used to load the workspace image.

It is also possible to save workspace images without quitting. For example, we could save all current workspace image information to a file called *temp.RData* by typing

```
> save.image("temp.RData")
```

Again, we can begin an R session with that workspace image, by clicking on the icon for *temp.RData*. Alternatively, we can type `load("temp.RData")` after entering an R session. Objects that were already in the current workspace image will remain, unless they have the same name as objects in the workspace image associated with *temp.RData*. In the latter case, the current objects will be overwritten and lost.

2.5.5 Data frames and the `read.table` function

Data sets frequently consist of more than one column of data, where each column represents measurements of a single variable. Each row usually represents a single observation. This format is referred to as *case-by-variable* format.

For example, the following data set consists of four observations on the three variables x, y, and z:

x	y	z
61	13	4
175	21	18
111	24	14
124	23	18

If such a data set is stored in a file called *pretend.dat* in the directory *myfiles* on the *C:* drive, then it can be read into an R data frame. This can be accomplished by typing

```
> pretend.df <- read.table("c:/myfiles/pretend.dat", header=T)
```

In a data frame, the columns are named. To see the x column, type

```
> pretend.df$x
```

2.5.6 Lists

Data frames are actually a special kind of list, or structure. Lists in R can contain any other objects. You won't often construct these yourself, but many functions return complicated results as lists. You can see the names of the objects in a list using the names () function, and extract parts of it:

```
> names(d)    # Print the names of the objects in the d data frame.
> d$x         # Print the x component of d
```

The list () function is one way of organizing multiple pieces of output from functions. For example,

```
> x <- c(3, 2, 3)
> y <- c(7, 7)
> list(x = x, y = y)
$x
[1] 3 2 3

$y
[1] 7 7
```

Exercises

1 Display the row 1, column 3 element of pretend.df.

2 Use two different commands to display the y column of pretend.df.

Chapter exercises

1 Assign the data set in *rnf6080.dat*[8] to a data frame called rain.df. Use the header=FALSE option.

    (a) Display the row 2, column 4 element of rain.df.

    (b) What are the names of the columns of rain.df.

    (c) Display the contents of the second row of the rain dataset.

    (d) Use the following command to re-label the columns of this data frame:

```
> names(rain.df) <- c("year", "month", "day", seq(0, 23))
```

    (e) Create a new column called daily which is the sum of the 24 hourly columns.

    (f) Plot a histogram of the daily rainfall amounts.

2 Plot the graph of the function

$$f(x) = \begin{cases} 3x + 2, & x \le 3 \\ 2x - 0.5x^2, & x > 3 \end{cases}$$

on the interval $[0, 6]$.

[8] This data set is available at www.stats.uwo.ca/faculty/braun/data/rnf6080.dat.

3

Programming statistical graphics

Users of statistical computing will need to produce graphs of their data and the results of their computations. In this chapter we start with a general overview of how this is done in R, and learn how to draw some basic plots. We then discuss some of the issues involved in *choosing* a style of plot to draw: it is not always an easy choice, and there are plenty of bad examples in the world to lead us astray. Finally, we will go into some detail about how to customize graphs in R.

There are several different graphics systems in R. The oldest one is most directly comparable to the original S graphics, and is now known as base graphics. You can think of base graphics as analogous to drawing with ink on paper. You build up a picture by drawing fixed things on it, and once something is drawn, it is permanent, though you might be able to cover it with something else, or move to a clean sheet of paper. Since the very beginning, base graphics has been designed to allow easy production of good quality scientific plots. In this chapter we will concentrate on base graphics.

The `grid` package provides the basis for a newer graphics system. It also has facilities to produce good quality graphics, but the programmer has access to the individual pieces of a graph, and can modify them: a graph is more like a physical model being built and displayed, rather than just drawn. The `lattice` and `ggplot` packages provide functions for high-level plots based on grid graphics.

Both base and grid graphics are designed to be "device independent." Directions are given where to draw and these drawing commands work on any device. The actual look of a graph will vary slightly from one device to another (e.g. on paper versus in a window on your screen), because of different capabilities.

There are other more exotic graphics systems available in R as well, providing interactive graphics, 3-D displays, etc. These are beyond the scope of this book.

3.1 | High-level plots

In this section we will discuss several basic plots. The functions to draw these in R are called "high level" because you don't need to worry about

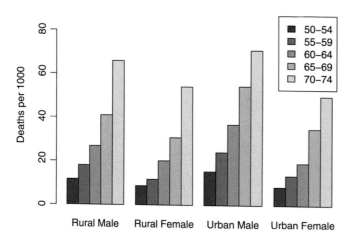

Fig. 3.1 An example of a bar chart.

the details of where the ink goes; you just describe the plot you want, and R does the drawing.

3.1.1 Bar charts and dot charts

The most basic type of graph is one that displays a single set of numbers. Bar charts and dot charts do this by displaying a bar or dot whose length or position corresponds to the number.

For example, the VADeaths dataset in R contains death rates (number of deaths per 1000 population per year) in various subpopulations within the state of Virginia in 1940. This may be plotted as a bar chart.

```
> VADeaths
      Rural Male Rural Female Urban Male Urban Female
50-54     11.7          8.7       15.4          8.4
55-59     18.1         11.7       24.3         13.6
60-64     26.9         20.3       37.0         19.3
65-69     41.0         30.9       54.6         35.1
70-74     66.0         54.3       71.1         50.0

> barplot(VADeaths, beside=TRUE, legend=TRUE, ylim=c(0, 90),
+          ylab="Deaths per 1000",
+          main="Death rates in Virginia")
```

Figure 3.1 shows the plot that results. The bars correspond to each number in the matrix. The beside=TRUE argument causes the values in each column to be plotted side-by-side; legend=TRUE causes the legend in the top right to be added. The ylim=c(0, 90) argument modifies the vertical scale of the graph to make room for the legend. (We will describe other ways to place the legend in Section 3.3 below.) Finally, the main=argument sets the main title for the plot.

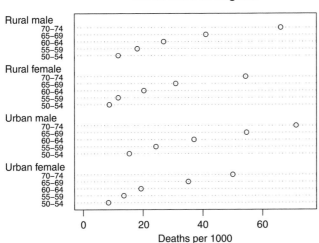

Death rates in Virginia

Fig. 3.2 An example of a dot chart.

An alternative way to plot the same data is in a dot chart (Figure 3.2).

```
> dotchart(VADeaths, xlim=c(0, 75),
+          xlab="Deaths per 1000",
+          main="Death rates in Virginia")
```

We set the x-axis limits to run from 0 to 75 so that zero is included, because it is natural to want to compare the total rates in the different groups.

3.1.2 Pie charts

Pie charts display a vector of numbers by breaking up a circular disk into pieces whose angle (and hence area) is proportional to each number. For example, the letter grades assigned to a class might arise in the proportions shown in Figure 3.3, which was drawn with the R code

Fig. 3.3 A pie chart showing the distribution of grades in a class.

```
> groupsizes <- c(18, 30, 32, 10, 10)
> labels <- c("A", "B", "C", "D", "F")
> pie(groupsizes, labels, col=c("grey40", "white", "grey", "black", "grey90"))
```

Pie charts are popular in non-technical publications, but they have fallen out of favour with statisticians. Some of the reasons why will be discussed in Section 3.2.

3.1.3 Histograms

A histogram is a special type of bar chart that is used to show the frequency distribution of a collection of numbers. Each bar represents the count of x values that fall in the range indicated by the base of the bar. Usually all bars should be the same width; this is the default in R. In this case the height of each bar is proportional to the number of observations in the corresponding interval. If bars have different widths, then the *area* of the bar should be proportional to the count; in this way the height represents the density (i.e. the frequency per unit of x).

Histogram of x

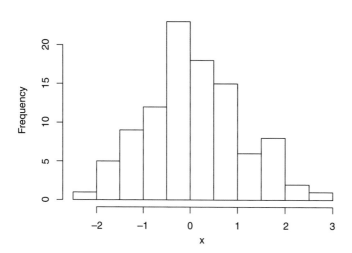

Fig. 3.4 An example of a histogram of the values in a vector x of length 100. We can see for example that the most frequently observed interval is −0.5 to 0, and that 23 values lie therein.

In R, hist(x, ...) is the main way to plot histograms. Here x is a vector consisting of numeric observations, and optional parameters in ... are used to control the details of the display. For example, Figure 3.4 shows the result of the following code.

```
> x <- rnorm(100)
> hist(x)
```

If you have n values of x, R, by default, divides the range into approximately $\log_2(n)+1$ intervals, giving rise to that number of bars. For example, our data set consisted of 100 measurements. Since

$$100 > 2^6 = 64$$

$$100 < 2^7 = 128$$

$$6 < \log_2(100) < 7,$$

it can be seen that R should choose about 7 or 8 bars. In fact, it chose 11, because it also attempts to put the breaks at round numbers (multiples of 0.5 in this case).

The above rule (known as the "Sturges" rule) is not always satisfactory for very large values of n, giving too few bars. Current research suggests that the number of bars should increase proportionally to $n^{1/3}$ rather than proportional to $\log_2(n)$. The breaks = "Scott" and breaks = "Freedman-Diaconis" options provide variations on this choice. For example, Figure 3.5 shows the results for a 10 000 point dataset using the "Sturges" and "Scott" rules.

3.1.4 Box plots

A box plot (or "box-and-whisker plot") is an alternative to a histogram to give a quick visual display of the main features of a set of data. A rectangular box is drawn, together with lines which protrude from two opposing sides.

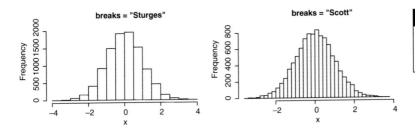

The box gives an indication of the location and spread of the central portion of the data, while the extent of the lines (the "whiskers") provides an idea of the range of the bulk of the data. In some implementations, outliers (observations that are very different from the rest of the data) are plotted as separate points.

The basic construction of the box part of the boxplot is as follows:

1 A horizontal line is drawn at the median.
2 Split the data into two halves, each containing the median.
3 Calculate the upper and lower quartiles as the medians of each half, and draw horizontal lines at each of these values. Then connect the lines to form a rectangular box.

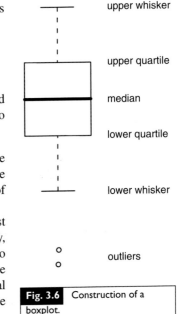

The box thus drawn defines the *interquartile range* (IQR). This is the difference between the upper quartile and the lower quartile. We use the IQR to give a measure of the amount of variability in the central portion of the dataset, since about 50% of the data will lie within the box.

The lower whisker is drawn from the lower end of the box to the smallest value that is no smaller than 1.5 IQR below the lower quartile. Similarly, the upper whisker is drawn from the middle of the upper end of the box to the largest value that is no larger than 1.5 IQR above the upper quartile. The rationale for these definitions is that when data are drawn from the normal distribution or other distributions with a similar shape, about 99% of the observations will fall between the whiskers.

Fig. 3.6 Construction of a boxplot.

An annotated example of a box plot is displayed in Figure 3.6. Box plots are convenient for comparing distributions of data in two or more categories, with a number (say 10 or more) of numerical observations per category. For example, the `iris` dataset in R is a well-studied dataset of measurements of 50 flowers from each of three species of iris. Figure 3.7, produced by the code

```
> boxplot(Sepal.Length ~ Species, data = iris,
+          ylab = "Sepal length (cm)", main = "Iris measurements",
+          boxwex = 0.5)
```

compares the distributions of the sepal length measurements between the different species. Here we have used R's formula based interface to the graphics function: the syntax `Sepal.Length ~ Species` is read as "Sepal.Length depending on Species," where both are columns of the data frame specified by `data = iris`. The `boxplot()` function draws separate side-by-side box plots for each species. From these, we can see

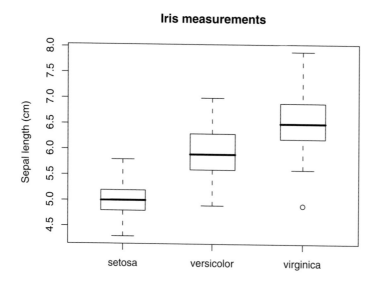

Iris measurements

Sepal length (cm)

setosa   versicolor   virginica

Fig. 3.7 An example of side-by-side boxplots.

substantial differences between the mean lengths for the species, and that there is one unusually small specimen among the *virginica* samples.

3.1.5 Scatterplots

When doing statistics, most of the interesting problems have to do with the relationships between different measurements. To study this, one of the most commonly used plots is the scatterplot, in which points (x_i, y_i), $i = 1, \ldots, n$ are drawn using dots or other symbols. These are drawn to show relationships between the x_i and y_i values. In R, scatterplots (and many other kinds of plots) are drawn using the `plot()` function. Its basic usage is `plot(x, y, ...)` where x and y are numeric vectors of the same length holding the data to be plotted. There are many additional optional arguments, and versions of `plot` designed for non-numerical data as well.

One important optional argument is `type`. The default is `type="p"`, which draws a scatterplot. Line plots (in which line segments join the (x_i, y_i) points in order from first to last) are drawn using `type="l"`. Many other types are available, including `type="n"`, to draw *nothing*: this just sets up the frame around the plot, allowing other functions to be used to draw in it. Some of these other functions will be discussed in Section 3.3.

Many other types of graphs can be obtained with this function. We will show how to explore some of the options using some artificial data. Two vectors of numbers will be simulated, one from a standard normal distribution and the other from a Poisson distribution having mean 30.

```
> x <- rnorm(100)        # assigns 100 random normal observations to x
> y <- rpois(100, 30)    # assigns 100 random Poisson observations
>                        # to y; mean value is 30
> mean(y)                # the resulting value should be near 30
[1] 30.91
```

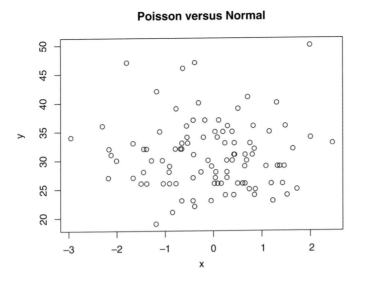

Poisson versus Normal

Fig. 3.8 An example of a scatterplot.

The `main` argument sets the main title for the plot. Figure 3.8 shows the result of

```
> plot(x, y, main = "Poisson versus Normal")
```

Other possibilities you should try:

```
> plot(x, y, type="l")    # plots a broken line (a dense tangle of line
>                         # segments here)
> plot(sort(x), sort(y), type="l")   # a plot of the sample "quantiles"
```

There are many more optional arguments to the `plot()` function, described on the `?plot` and `?par` help pages.

3.1.6 QQ plots

Quantile–quantile plots (otherwise known as QQ plots) are a type of scatterplot used to compare the distributions of two groups or to compare a sample with a reference distribution.

In the case where there are two groups of equal size, the QQ plot is obtained by first sorting the observations in each group: $X[1] \leq \cdots \leq X[n]$ and $Y[1] \leq \cdots \leq Y[n]$. Next, draw a scatterplot of $(X[i], Y[i])$, for $i = 1, \ldots, n$.

When the groups are of different sizes, some scheme must be used to artificially match them. R reduces the size of the larger group to the size of the smaller one by keeping the minimum and maximum values, and choosing equally spaced quantiles between. For example, if there were five X values but twenty Y values, then the X values would be plotted against the minimum, lower quartile, median, upper quartile and maximum of the Y values.

When plotting a single sample against a reference distribution, theoretical quantiles are used for one coordinate. R normally puts the theoretical quantiles on the X axis and the data on the Y axis, but some authors make the opposite choice. To avoid biases, quantiles are chosen corresponding to probabilities $(i - 1/2)/n$: these are centered evenly between zero and one.

When the distributions of X and Y match, the points in the QQ plot will lie near the line $y = x$. We will see a different straight line if one distribution is a linear transformation of the other. On the other hand, if the two distributions are not the same, we will see systematic patterns in the QQ plot. The following code illustrates some common patterns (see Figure 3.9).

```
> X <- rnorm(1000)
> A <- rnorm(1000)
> qqplot(X, A, main="A and X are the same")
> B <- rnorm(1000, mean=3, sd=2)
> qqplot(X, B, main="B is rescaled X")
> C <- rt(1000, df=2)
> qqplot(X, C, main="C has heavier tails")
> D <- exp(rnorm(1000))
> qqplot(X, D, main="D is skewed to the right")
```

Exercises

1 The `islands` vector contains the areas of 48 land masses.
   (a) Plot a histogram of these data.
   (b) Are there advantages to taking logarithms of the areas before plotting the histogram?
   (c) Compare the histograms that result when using breaks based on Sturges' and Scott's rules. Make this comparison on the log-scale and on the original scale.
   (d) Construct a boxplot for these data on the log-scale as well as the original scale.
   (d) Construct a dot-chart of the areas. Is a log transformation needed here?
   (f) Which form of graphic do you think is most appropriate for displaying these data?

2 The `stackloss` data frame contains 21 observations on four variables taken at a factory where ammonia is converted to nitric acid. The first three variables are `Air.Flow`, `Water.Temp`, and `Acid.Conc`. The fourth variable is `stack.loss`, which measures the amount of ammonia that escapes before being absorbed. (Read the help file for more information about this data frame.)
   (a) Use scatterplots to explore possible relationships between acid concentration, water temperature, and air flow and the amount of ammonia which escapes. Do these relationships appear to be linear or nonlinear?
   (b) Use the `pairs()` function to obtain all pairwise scatterplots among the four variables. Identify pairs of variables where there might be linear or nonlinear relationships.

3 Consider the `pressure` data frame. There are two columns: `temperature` and `pressure`.

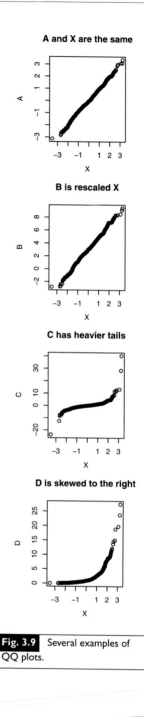

Fig. 3.9 Several examples of QQ plots.

(a) Construct a scatterplot with `pressure` on the vertical axis and `temperature` on the horizontal axis. Are the variables related linearly or nonlinearly?

(b) The graph of the following function passes through the plotted points reasonably well:

$$y = (0.168 + 0.007x)^{20/3}.$$

The differences between the pressure values predicted by the curve and the observed pressure values are called *residuals*. Here is a way to calculate them:

```
> residuals <-with(pressure, pressure-(0.168+0.007*temperature)^(20/3))
```

Construct a normal QQ-plot of these residuals and decide whether they are normally distributed or whether they follow a skewed distribution.

(c) Now, apply the power transformation $y^{3/20}$ to the pressure data values. Plot these transformed values against temperature. Is a linear or nonlinear relationship evident now?

(d) Calculate residuals for the difference between transformed pressure values and those predicted by the straight line. Obtain a normal QQ-plot, and decide whether the residuals follow a normal distribution or not.

3.2 | Choosing a high-level graphic

We have described bar, dot, and pie charts, histograms, box plots, scatterplots, and QQ plots. There are many other styles of statistical graphics that we haven't discussed. How should a user choose which one to use?

The first consideration is the type of data. As discussed in the previous section, bar, dot, and pie charts display individual values, histograms, box plots, and QQ plots display distributions, and scatterplots display pairs of values.

Another consideration is the audience. If the plot is for yourself or for a statistically educated audience, then you can assume a more sophisticated understanding. For example, a box plot or QQ plot would require more explanation than a histogram, and might not be appropriate for the general public.

It is also important to have some understanding of how human visual perception works in order to make a good choice. There has been a huge amount of research on this and we can only touch on it here.

When looking at a graph, you extract quantitative information when your visual system *decodes* the graph. This process can be described in terms of unconscious measurements of lengths, positions, slopes, angles, areas, volumes, and various aspects of color. It has been found that people are particularly good at recognizing lengths and positions, not as good at slopes and angles, and their perception of areas and volumes can be quite inaccurate, depending on the shape. Most of us are quite good at recognizing differences in colors. However, up to 10% of men and a much smaller proportion of women are partially color-blind, and almost nobody is very good at making quantitative measurements from colors.

We can take these facts about perception into account when we construct graphs. We should try to convey the important information in ways that are easy to perceive, and we should try not to have conflicting messages in a graph.

For example, the bars in bar charts are easy to recognize, because the position of the ends of the bars and the length of the bars are easy to see. The area of the bars also reinforces our perception.

However, the fact that we see length and area when we look at a bar constrains us. We should normally base bar charts at zero, so that the position, length and area all convey the same information. If we are displaying numbers where zero is not relevant, then a dot chart is a better choice: in a dot chart it is mainly the position of the dot that is perceived.

Thinking in terms of visual tasks tells us that pie charts can be poor choices for displaying data. In order to see the sizes of slices of the pie, we need to make angle and area measurements, and we are not very good at those.

Finally, color can be very useful in graphs to distinguish groups from each other. The `RColorBrewer` package in R contains a number of *palettes*, or selections of colors. Some palettes indicate sequential groups from low to high, others show groups that diverge from a neutral value, and others are purely qualitative. These are chosen so that most people (even if color-blind) can easily see the differences.

3.3 | Low-level graphics functions

Functions like `barplot()`, `dotchart()` and `plot()` do their work by using low-level graphics functions to draw lines and points, to establish where they will be placed on a page, and so on.

In this section we will describe some of these low-level functions, which are also available to users to customize their plots. We will start with a description of how R views the page it is drawing on, then show how to add points, lines, and text to existing plots, and finish by showing how some of the common graphics settings are changed.

3.3.1 The plotting region and margins

Base graphics in R divides up the display into several regions. The plot region is where data will be drawn. Within the plot region R maintains a coordinate system based on the data. The axes show this coordinate system. Outside the plot region are the margins, numbered clockwise from 1 to 4, starting at the bottom. Normally text and labels are plotted in the margins, and R positions objects based on a count of lines out from the plot region. Figure 3.10 illustrates this. (We give the code that produced this plot below.)

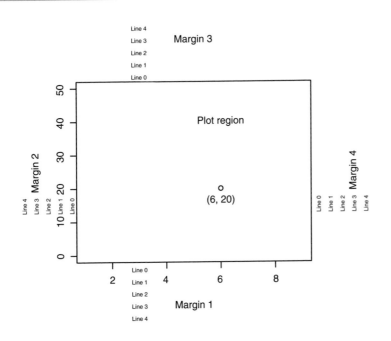

Fig. 3.10 The plotting region in base graphics.

We can see from the figure that R chose to draw the tick mark labels on line 1. We drew the margin titles on line 3.

3.3.2 Adding to plots

Several functions exist to add components to the plot region of existing graphs:

- `points(x, y, ...)`
- `lines(x, y, ...)` adds line segments
- `text(x, y, labels, ...)` adds text into the graph
- `abline(a, b, ...)` adds the line $y = a + bx$
- `abline(h=y, ...)` adds a horizontal line
- `abline(v=x, ...)` adds a vertical line
- `polygon(x, y, ...)` adds a closed and possibly filled polygon
- `segments(x0, y0, x1, y1, ...)` draws line segments
- `arrows(x0, y0, x1, y1, ...)` draws arrows
- `symbols(x, y, ...)` draws circles, squares, thermometers, etc.
- `legend(x, y, legend, ...)` draws a legend.

The optional arguments to these functions specify the color, size, and other characteristics of the items being added.

For example, we will use measurements on the lengths and widths (in cm) of the left index finger for a random sample of eight adult individuals. The data are stored in a data frame called `indexfinger` which is displayed below.

```
> indexfinger
  sex length width
1   M    7.9   2.3
2   F    6.5   1.7
```

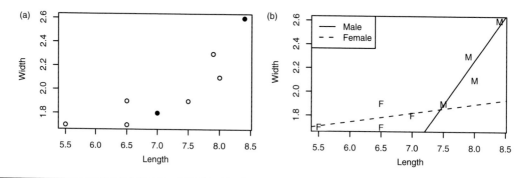

Fig. 3.11 A scatter plot of finger width versus finger length for eight individuals. (a): Highlighting two points. (b): Using different plot characters for each sex.

3	M	8.4	2.6
4	F	5.5	1.7
5	F	6.5	1.9
6	M	8.0	2.1
7	F	7.0	1.8
8	M	7.5	1.9

We can create a simple scatter plot of these data illustrating the relation between length and width using

```
> plot(width ~ length, data=indexfinger)
```

Suppose that after plotting this figure, we decide to highlight the male and female with the longest fingers (observations 3 and 7). We will use the points() function to plot additional points on the graph on top of the original ones with the following code:[1]

```
> with(indexfinger[c(3, 7),], points(length, width, pch=16))
```

The result is shown in Figure 3.11(a). The pch=16 argument changes the plotting character from the default open circle to a solid black dot. Other numerical values of this parameter will give different plotting characters. We can also ask for different characters to be plotted; for example, pch="f" causes R to plot the letter f.

[1] The with () function allows us to access columns of a data frame directly without using the $ convention. See help (with) for more information.

Another possibility would be to specify the pch value in the original call to plot(), for example

```
> plot(width ~ length, pch=as.character(sex), data=indexfinger)
```

We could then add linear regression lines for the males and the females, and a legend to identify them.

```
> abline(lm(width ~ length, data=indexfinger, subset=sex=="M"), lty=1)
> abline(lm(width ~ length, data=indexfinger, subset=sex=="F"), lty=2)
> legend("topleft", legend=c("Male", "Female"), lty=1:2)
```

Figure 3.11(b) shows the results.

One may also wish to annotate graphs outside the plot region. Several functions exist to do this:

- `title(main, sub, xlab, ylab, ...)` adds a main title, a subtitle, an *x*-axis label and/or a *y*-axis label
- `mtext(text, side, line, ...)` draws text in the margins
- `axis(side, at, labels, ...)` adds an axis to the plot
- `box(...)` adds a box around the plot region.

For example, Figure 3.10 was drawn using the following code:

```
> par(mar=c(5, 5, 5, 5) + 0.1)
> plot(c(1, 9), c(0, 50), type="n", xlab="", ylab="")
> text(6, 40, "Plot region")
> points(6, 20)
> text(6, 20, "(6, 20)", adj=c(0.5, 2))
> mtext(paste("Margin", 1:4), side=1:4, line=3)
> mtext(paste("Line", 0:4), side=1, line=0:4, at=3, cex=0.6)
> mtext(paste("Line", 0:4), side=2, line=0:4, at=15, cex=0.6)
> mtext(paste("Line", 0:4), side=3, line=0:4, at=3, cex=0.6)
> mtext(paste("Line", 0:4), side=4, line=0:4, at=15, cex=0.6)
```

We discuss the `par()` function in the next section.

3.3.3 Setting graphical parameters

When creating a new plot, there are two opportunities to set its overall characteristics. The first is when the plotting device is opened. R normally opens a screen device automatically with default parameters, but a user can open a plotting device explicitly, and set it up exactly as required. The availability of these depends on the platform on which you are working. Some plotting devices in R are:

- `windows(...)` to open a screen device in MS Windows
- `x11(...)` or `X11(...)` to open a screen device in Unix-alike systems
- `quartz(...)` to open a screen device in Mac OSX
- `postscript(...)` to open a file for Postscript output for printing
- `pdf(...)` to open a file for PDF output
- `jpeg(...)` to open a file for JPEG bitmap output
- `png(...)` to open a file for PNG bitmap output.

You will need to read the help pages for each of these functions to find out the exact details of the available parameters. They control things like the size of the plot, background colors, and so on.

After a device is opened, other graphical parameters may be set using the `par(...)` function. This function controls a very large number of parameters; we will just highlight a few here. For the complete list, see the help page.

- `mfrow=c(m, n)` tells R to draw m rows and n columns of plots, rather than going to a new page for each plot.
- `mfg=c(i, j)` says to draw the figure in row i and column j next.
- `ask=TRUE` tells R to ask the user before erasing a plot to draw a new one.

- `cex=1.5` tells R to expand characters by this amount in the plot region. There are separate `cex.axis`, etc. parameters to control text in the margins.
- `mar=c(side1, side2, side3, side4)` sets the margins of the plot to the given numbers of lines of text on each side.
- `oma=c(side1, side2, side3, side4)` sets the outer margins (the region outside the array of plots).
- `usr=c(x1, x2, y1, y2)` sets the coordinate system within the plot with x and y coordinates on the given ranges.

The `par()` function is set up to take arguments in several forms. If you give character strings (e.g. `par("mfrow")`), the function will return the current value of the graphical parameter. If you provide named arguments (e.g. `par(mfrow=c(1, 2))`), you will set the corresponding parameter, and the previous value will be returned in a `list`. Finally, you can use a `list` as input to set several parameters at once.

Chapter exercises

1 Consider the `islands` data set again. In particular, try out the following code.

```
> hist(log(islands,10), breaks="Scott", axes=FALSE, xlab="area",
+                        main="Histogram of Island Areas")
> axis(1, at=1:5, labels=10^(1:5))
> axis(2)
> box()
```

(a) Explain what is happening at each step of the above code.
(b) Add a subtitle to the plot such as "Base-10 Log-Scale."
(c) Modify the code to incorporate the use of the Sturges rule in place of the Scott rule. In this case, you will need to use the `round()` function to ensure that excessive numbers of digits are not used in the axis labels.

2 Consider the `pressure` data frame again.

(a) Plot `pressure` against `temperature`, and use the following command to pass a curve through these data:

```
> curve((0.168 + 0.007*x)^(20/3), from=0, to=400, add=TRUE)
```

(b) Now, apply the power transformation $y^{3/20}$ to the pressure data values. Plot these transformed values against temperature. Is a linear or nonlinear relationship evident now? Use the `abline()` function to pass a straight line through the points. (You need an intercept and slope for this – see the previous part of this question to obtain appropriate values.)
(c) Add a suitable title to the graph.
(d) Re-do the above plots, but use the `mfrow()` function to display them in a 2 × 1 layout on the graphics page. Repeat once again using a 1 × 2 layout.

4

Programming with R

Programming involves writing relatively complex systems of instructions. There are two broad styles of programming: the imperative style (used in R, for example) involves stringing together instructions telling the computer what to do. The declarative style (used in HTML in web pages, for example) involves writing a description of the end result, without giving the details about how to get there. Within each of these broad styles, there are many subdivisions, and a given program may involve aspects of several of them. For example, R programs may be procedural (describing what steps to take to achieve a task), modular (broken up into self-contained packages), object-oriented (organized to describe operations on complex objects), functional (organized as a collection of functions which do specific calculations without having external side-effects), among other possibilities. In this book we will concentrate on the procedural aspects of programming.

As described in Chapter 1, R statements mainly consist of expressions to be evaluated. Most programs are very repetitive, but the amount of repetition depends on the input. In this chapter we start by describing several *flow control* statements that control how many times statements are repeated. The remainder of the chapter gives advice on how to design and debug programs.

4.1 | Flow control

4.1.1 The for() loop
One of the goals of this book is to introduce stochastic simulation. Simulations are often very repetitive: we want to see patterns of behaviour, not just a single instance.

The for() statement allows one to specify that a certain operation should be repeated a fixed number of times.

Syntax
```
for (name in vector)    {commands}
```

This sets a variable called name equal to each of the elements of vector, in sequence. For each value, whatever commands are listed within the curly braces will be performed. The curly braces serve to group the commands so that they are treated by R as a single command. If there is only one command to execute, the braces are not needed.

Example 4.1

The Fibonacci sequence is a famous sequence in mathematics. The first two elements are defined as [1, 1]. Subsequent elements are defined as the sum of the preceding two elements. For example, the third element is 2 ($= 1+1$), the fourth element is 3 ($= 1+2$), the fifth element is 5 ($= 2+3$), and so on.

To obtain the first 12 Fibonacci numbers in R, we can use

```
> Fibonacci <- numeric(12)
> Fibonacci[1] <- Fibonacci[2] <- 1
> for (i in 3:12) Fibonacci[i] <- Fibonacci[i - 2] + Fibonacci[i - 1]
```

Understanding the code

The first line sets up a numeric vector of length 12 with the name Fibonacci. This vector consists of 12 zeroes. The second line updates the first two elements of Fibonacci to the value 1. The third line updates the third element, fourth element, and so on according to the rule defining the Fibonacci sequence. In particular, Fibonacci[3] is assigned the value of Fibonacci[1] + Fibonacci[2], i.e. 2. Fibonacci[4] is then assigned the latest value of Fibonacci[2] + Fibonacci[3], giving it the value 3. The for() loop updates the third through 12th element of the sequence in this way.

To see all 12 values, type in

```
> Fibonacci
[1]   1   1   2   3   5   8  13  21  34  55  89 144
```

Example 4.2

Suppose a car dealer promotes two options for the purchase of a new $20 000 car. The first option is for the customer to pay up front and receive a $1000 rebate. The second option is "0%-interest financing" where the customer makes 20 monthly payments of $1000 beginning in one month's time.

Because of option 1, the effective price of the car is really $19 000, so the dealer really is charging some interest rate i for option 2. We can calculate this value using the formula for the present value of an annuity:

$$19\,000 = 1000 \left(\frac{1 - (1 + i)^{-20}}{i} \right).$$

By multiplying both sides of this equation by i and dividing by $19\,000$, we get the form of a *fixed-point* problem:[1]

$$i = \frac{(1 - (1 + i)^{-20})}{19}.$$

By taking an initial guess for i and plugging it into the right-hand side of this equation, we can get an 'updated' value for i on the left. For example, if we start with $i = 0.006$, then our update is

$$i = \frac{(1 - (1 + 0.006)^{-20})}{19} = 0.005\,93.$$

By plugging this updated value into the right-hand side of the equation again, we get a new update:

$$i = \frac{(1 - (1 + 0.005\,93)^{-20})}{19} = 0.005\,86.$$

This kind of fixed-point iteration usually requires many iterations before we can be confident that we have the solution to the fixed-point equation. Here is R code to work out the solution after 1000 iterations:

```
> i <- 0.006
> for (j in 1:1000) {
+     i <- (1 - (1 + i)^(-20)) / 19
+ }
> i
[1] 0.004 935 593
```

Exercises

1 Modify the code to generate the Fibonacci sequence in the following ways:
   (a) Change the first two elements to 2 and 2.
   (b) Change the first two elements to 3 and 2.
   (c) Change the update rule from summing successive elements to taking differences of successive elements. For example, the third element is defined as the second element minus the first element, and so on.
   (d) Change the update rule so that each element is defined as the sum of three preceding elements. Set the third element as 1 in order to start the process.

2 Let f_n denote the nth Fibonacci number.
   (a) Construct a sequence of ratios of the form $f_n/f_{n-1}, n = 1, 2, \ldots, 30$. Does the sequence appear to be converging?
   (b) Compute the golden ratio $(1 + \sqrt{5})/2$. Is the sequence converging to this ratio? Can you prove this?

3 In each of the following, determine the final value of `answer`. Check your result by running the code in R.
   (a)
```
> answer <- 0
> for (j in 1:5) answer <- answer + j
```

[1] A fixed-point problem arises when we want to solve an equation of the form $x = f(x)$, for some function $f(x)$. Note that the unknown value is on both sides of the equation.

(b) > answer <- NULL
     > for (j in 1:5) answer <- c(answer, j)
(c) > answer <- 0
     > for (j in 1:5) answer <- c(answer, j)
(d) > answer <- 1
     > for (j in 1:5) answer <- answer * j
(e) > answer <- 3
     > for (j in 1:15) answer <- c(answer, (7 * answer[j]) %% 31)

Inspect this last sequence of numbers. If you did not know the rule used to determine this sequence, would you be able to predict successive elements?

4 Refer to the car dealer promotion example in this section. Calculate the first 20 updates of the interest rate i, starting with $i = 0.006$. Repeat with a starting value of $i = 0.005$, and with a starting value of $i = 0.004$. Based on these observations, what is the true value of i (up to five-digit accuracy)?

5 Use a fixed-point iteration to determine the solution (in $[0, 1]$) of the equation $x = \cos(x)$. Use a starting value of 0.5. How many iterations does it take before you have an answer which is accurate in the first two digits? ...in the first three digits? ...in the first four digits? What happens if you change the starting value to 0.7? ...to 0.0?

6 Repeat the previous question, but using the equation $x = 1.5\cos(x)$. (The solution is near $x = 0.914\,856\,5$.)

(a) Does the fixed-point iteration converge? If not, modify the equation so that $x = \cos(x)/30 + 44x/45$. Does the iteration converge now?

(b) Can you show that the solutions to these two equations are the same?

(c) Compute the absolute value of the derivative of $1.5\cos(x)$ and of $\cos(x)/30+44x/45$. There is a theorem in numerical analysis which says that if this quantity is less than 1, then the fixed-point iteration will converge if the starting guess is close enough to the solution. Does this explain the behavior that you observed in part (a)?

4.1.2 The if() statement

Earlier, we learned about logical vectors and relational operators. The subscripting device is a powerful way to perform different operations on different parts of vectors. The if() statement allows us to control which statements are executed, and sometimes this is more convenient.

Syntax

```
if (condition) {commands when TRUE}
if (condition) {commands when TRUE} else {commands when FALSE}
```

This statement causes a set of commands to be invoked if condition evaluates to TRUE. The else part is optional, and provides an alternative set of commands which are to be invoked in case the logical variable is FALSE. Be careful how you type this. Typing it as

```
if (condition) {commands when TRUE}
else {commands when FALSE}
```

may be an error, because R will execute the first line before you have time to enter the second. If these two lines appear within a block of commands in curly braces, they won't trigger an error, because R will collect all the lines before it starts to act on any of them.

To avoid ambiguities such as this, a common convention for typing if ... else is

```
if  (condition) {
     commands when TRUE
} else {
     commands when FALSE
}
```

When typed in this form, it is very clear that the statement is incomplete until the very end.

R also allows numerical values to be used as the value of condition. These are converted to logical values using the rule that zero becomes FALSE, and any other value becomes TRUE. Missing values are not allowed for the condition, and will trigger an error.

Example 4.3
A simple example:

```
> x <- 3
> if (x > 2) y <- 2 * x else y <- 3 * x
```

Since x > 2 is TRUE, y is assigned 2 * 3 = 6. If it hadn't been true, y would have been assigned the value of 3 * x.

The if() statement is often used inside user-defined functions. The following is a typical example.

Example 4.4
The correlation between two vectors of numbers is often calculated using the cor() function. It is supposed to give a measure of linear association. We can add a scatter plot of the data as follows:

```
> corplot <- function(x, y, plotit) {
+      if (plotit == TRUE) plot(x, y)
+      cor(x, y)
+ }
```

We can apply this function to two vectors without plotting by typing

```
> corplot(c(2, 5, 7), c(5, 6, 8), FALSE)
[1] 0.953821
```

Example 4.5

The function that follows is based on the sieve of Eratosthenes, the oldest known systematic method for listing prime numbers up to a given value *n*. The idea is as follows: begin with a vector of numbers from 2 to *n*. Beginning with 2, eliminate all multiples of 2 which are larger than 2. Then move to the next number remaining in the vector, in this case, 3. Now, remove all multiples of 3 which are larger than 3. Proceed through all remaining entries of the vector in this way. The entry for 4 would have been removed in the first round, leaving 5 as the next entry to work with after 3; all multiples of 5 would be removed at the next step and so on.

```
> Eratosthenes <- function(n) {
+   # Return all prime numbers up to n (based on the sieve of Eratosthenes)
+   if (n >= 2) {
+       sieve <- seq(2, n)
+       primes <- c()
+       for (i in seq(2, n)) {
+           if (any(sieve == i)) {
+               primes <- c(primes, i)
+               sieve <- c(sieve[(sieve %% i) != 0], i)
+           }
+       }
+       return(primes)
+   } else {
+       stop("Input value of n should be at least 2.")
+   }
+ }
```

Here are a couple of examples of the use of this function:

```
> Eratosthenes(50)
 [1]  2  3  5  7 11 13 17 19 23 29 31 37 41 43 47
> Eratosthenes(-50)
Error in Eratosthenes(-50) : Input value of n should be at least 2.
```

Understanding the code

The purpose of the function is to provide all prime numbers up to the given value n. The basic idea of the program is contained in the lines:

```
sieve <- seq(2, n)
primes <- c()
for (i in seq(2, n)) {
    if (any(sieve == i)) {
        primes <- c(primes, i)
        sieve <- sieve[(sieve %% i) != 0]
    }
}
```

The sieve object holds all the candidates for testing. Initially, all integers from 2 through n are stored in this vector. The primes object is set up initially empty, eventually to contain all of the primes that are less than or equal to n. The composite numbers in `sieve` are removed, and the primes are copied to `primes`.

Each integer `i` from 2 through `n` is checked in sequence to see whether it is still in the vector. The `any()` function returns a TRUE if at least one of the logical vector elements in its argument is TRUE. In the case that `i` is still in the `sieve` vector, it must be a prime, since it is the smallest number that has not been eliminated yet. All multiples of `i` are eliminated, since they are necessarily composite, and `i` is appended to `primes`. The expression `(sieve %% i) == 0` would give TRUE for all elements of `sieve` which are multiples of `i`; since we want to eliminate these elements and save all other elements, we can negate this using `!(sieve %% i == 0)` or `sieve %% i != 0`. Then we can eliminate all multiples of `i` from the `sieve` vector using

```
sieve <- sieve[(sieve %% i) != 0]
```

Note that this eliminates `i` as well, but we have already saved it in `primes`.

If the supplied argument `n` is less than 2, then the function output would be meaningless. To avoid this, we cause an error to be triggered if a value smaller than 2 is supplied by the user.

Exercises

1 Does the `Eratosthenes()` function work properly if `n` is not an integer? Is an error message required in this case?

2 Use the idea of the `Eratosthenes()` function to prove that there are infinitely many primes. *Hint:* Suppose all primes were less than m, and construct a larger value n that would not be eliminated by the sieve.

3 A twin prime is a pair of primes (x, y), such that $y = x + 2$. Construct a list of all twin primes below 1000.[2]

4 A bank offers a guaranteed investment certificate (GIC) which pays an annual interest rate of 4% (compounded annually) if the term is 3 years or less, or 5% if the term is more than 3 years. Write a function which takes the initial investment amount, P, and the number of interest periods (i.e. years) as arguments and which returns the amount of interest earned over the term of the GIC. That is, return I, where $I = P((1 + i)^n - 1)$.

5 Mortgage interest rates can sometimes depend on whether the mortgage term is *open* or *closed*. Use the formula

$$R = \frac{Pi}{1 - (1 + i)^{-n}}$$

to create a function to calculate a monthly mortgage payment R where i is an interest rate (compounded monthly), P is the original principal, and n is the length of the term (in months). The function should take n, P, and open as arguments. If open==TRUE, then take $i = 0.005$; otherwise, take $i = 0.004$.

[2] It has been known since ancient times that there are infinitely many primes. It remains a conjecture as to whether there is an infinite set of twin primes.

4.1.3 The while() loop

Sometimes we want to repeat statements, but the pattern of repetition isn't known in advance. We need to do some calculations and keep going as long as a condition holds. The while() statement accomplishes this.

Syntax

```
while (condition) {statements}
```

The condition is evaluated, and if it evaluates to FALSE, nothing more is done. If it evaluates to TRUE the statements are executed, condition is evaluated again, and the process is repeated.

Example 4.6

Suppose we want to list all Fibonacci numbers less than 300. We don't know beforehand how long this list is, so we wouldn't know how to stop the for() loop at the right time, but a while() loop is perfect:

```
> Fib1 <- 1
> Fib2 <- 1
> Fibonacci <- c(Fib1, Fib2)
> while (Fib2 < 300) {
+       Fibonacci <- c(Fibonacci, Fib2)
+       oldFib2 <- Fib2
+       Fib2 <- Fib1 + Fib2
+       Fib1 <- oldFib2
+ }
```

Understanding the code

The central idea is contained in the lines

```
while (Fib2 < 300) {
      Fibonacci <- c(Fibonacci, Fib2)
```

That is, as long as the latest Fibonacci number created (in Fib2) is less than 300, it is appended to the growing vector Fibonacci.

Thus, we must ensure that Fib2 actually contains the updated Fibonacci number. By keeping track of the two most recently added numbers (Fib1 and Fib2), we can do the update

```
Fib2 <- Fib1 + Fib2
```

Now Fib1 should be updated to the old value of Fib2, but that has been overwritten by the new value. So before executing the above line, we make a copy of Fib2 in oldFib2. After updating Fib2, we can assign the value in oldFib2 to Fib1.

In order to start things off, Fib1, Fib2, and Fibonacci need to be initialized. That is, within the loop, these objects will be used, so they need to be assigned sensible starting values.

To see the final result of the computation, type

```
> Fibonacci
 [1]   1   1   1   2   3   5   8  13  21  34  55  89 144 233
```

Caution
Increasing the length of a vector element by element as in
`Fibonacci<- c(Fibonacci, Fib2)` in a `for()` or `while()` loop
should be avoided if the number of such operations is likely to be large. R
will have to keep allocating new vectors, each one element longer than the
last one, and this will slow the process down substantially.

Exercises
1 The variable `oldFib2` isn't strictly necessary. Rewrite the Fibonacci
  `while()` loop with the update of `Fib1` based just on the current values
  of `Fib1` and `Fib2`.
2 In fact, `Fib1` and `Fib2` aren't necessary either. Rewrite the Fibonacci
  `while()` loop without using *any* variables except `Fibonacci`.
3 Determine the number of Fibonacci numbers less than 1 000 000.
4 Recall the car dealer interest rate example in Section 4.2. Use a
  `while()` loop to iteratively calculate the interest rate i which satisfies
  the fixed-point equation

$$i = \left(1 - (1 + i)^{-20}\right)/19.$$

  Use a starting guess of $i = 0.006$. Stop the calculation when two
  successive values of the interest rate are less than 0.000 001 apart.
  What happens when you try other starting guesses?
5 Referring to the previous exercise, modify your code so that it also
  computes the number of iterations required to get two successive values
  of the interest rate that are less than 0.000 001 apart.

4.1.4 Newton's method for root finding
Newton's method is a popular numerical method to find a root of an
algebraic equation:[3]

$$f(x) = 0.$$

If $f(x)$ has derivative $f'(x)$, then the following iteration will converge to a
root of the above equation if started close enough to the root.

$$x_0 = \text{initial guess}$$

$$x_n = x_{n-1} - \frac{f(x_{n-1})}{f'(x_{n-1})}.$$

The idea is based on the Taylor approximation

$$f(x_n) \approx f(x_{n-1}) + (x_n - x_{n-1})f'(x_{n-1}). \qquad (4.1)$$

[3] Alternatively, we say that it is finding
a zero of the function $f(x)$.

Newton's method is equivalent to setting $f(x_n) = 0$ and solving for x_n in (4.1). Even though (4.1) is only an approximation, we hope that the solution x_n should give a close approximation to the root. Be careful: there are many examples where x_n will fail to converge to a root unless x_{n-1} is already sufficiently close, and some where it will fail regardless of the starting value.

Example 4.7

Suppose $f(x) = x^3 + 2x^2 - 7$. Then, if x_0 is close enough to one of the three roots of this equation,

$$x_n = x_{n-1} - \frac{x_{n-1}^3 + 2x_{n-1}^2 - 7}{3x^2 + 4x}$$

will converge to a root.

An R version of this could be implemented as follows:

```
> x <- x0
> f <- x^3 + 2 * x^2 - 7
> tolerance <- 0.000001
> while (abs(f) > tolerance) {
+       f.prime <- 3 * x^2 + 4 * x
+       x <- x - f / f.prime
+       f <- x^3 + 2 * x^2 - 7
+ }
> x
```

Understanding the code

We start with x equal to x_0, and evaluate $f(x_0)$. Then, as long as $|f(x_i)|$ is more than 0.000001, we update x using Newton's method. Notice that we don't need a variable i. Because Newton's method is a recursive formula where the new value can be calculated from the old one, there is no need to know which iteration we are on when doing the updates.

Exercises

1 The equation

$$x^7 + 10\,000x^6 + 1.06x^5 + 10\,600x^4 + 0.0605x^3 + 605x^2 + 0.0005x + 5$$

has exactly one real root. How many iterations of Newton's method are required to find this root if the initial guess is $x = 0$?

2 Use Newton's method to find a zero of

$$f(x) = x^4 + 3x^3 - 2x^2 - 7,$$

using an initial guess of $x = 1$.

3 Modify the above function so that it finds one of the zeros of

$$f(x) = \cos(x) + e^x,$$

using an initial guess of $x = -1.5$.

4 Find a minimizer of the function

$$f(x) = (x-3)^4 + 7(x-2)^2 + x.$$

5 How many zeros does the function

$$f(x) = \frac{5x-3}{x-1}$$

have? What are they? Describe the behavior of Newton's method applied to this function if the initial guess is
(a) 0.5
(b) 0.75
(c) 0.2
(d) 1.25.

6 How many zeros does the function

$$f(x) = (x^2 - 6x + 9)e^{-x}$$

have? What are they? Describe the behavior of Newton's method applied to this function if the initial guess is
(a) 3
(b) 3.2
(c) 2.99
(d) 3.01.

7 Refer to the car dealer interest rate example in Section 4.2. Use Newton's method to calculate the interest rate i which satisfies

$$i = \left(1 - (1+i)^{-20}\right)/19.$$

Use $i = 0.006$ as your starting guess. How many iterations are required for two successive values of i to be within 0.000 001 of each other?

4.1.5 The `repeat` loop, and the `break` and `next` statements

Sometimes we don't want a fixed number of repetitions of a loop, and we don't want to put the test at the top of the loop the way it is in a `while()` loop. In this situation we can use a `repeat` loop. This loop repeats until we execute a `break` statement.

Syntax
```
repeat { statements }
```

This causes the statements to be repeated endlessly. The statements should normally include a `break` statement, typically in the form

```
if (condition) break
```

but this is not a requirement of the syntax.

The `break` statement causes the loop to terminate immediately. `break` statements can also be used in `for()` and `while()` loops. The `next` statement causes control to return immediately to the top of the loop; it can also be used in any loop.

The repeat loop and the break and next statements are used relatively infrequently. It is usually easier to understand code when the test is clearly displayed at the top, and when that is the only exit from the loop (as in the for and while loops). However, sometimes these statements help to make programs clearer.

Example 4.8

We can repeat the Newton's algorithm example from the previous section using a repeat loop:

```
> x <- x0
> tolerance <- 0.000001
> repeat {
+        f <- x^3 + 2 * x^2 - 7
+        if (abs(f) < tolerance) break
+        f.prime <- 3 * x^2 + 4 * x
+        x <- x - f / f.prime
+ }
> x
```

This version removes the need to duplicate the line that calculates f.

Exercises

1 Another algorithm for finding a zero of a function is called the *bisection algorithm*. This algorithm starts with two values x_1 and x_2 for which $f(x_1)$ and $f(x_2)$ have opposite signs. If $f(x)$ is a continuous function, then we know a root must lie somewhere between these two values. We find it by evaluating $f(x)$ at the midpoint, and selecting whichever half of the interval still brackets the root. We then start over, and repeat the calculation until the interval is short enough to give us our answer to the required precision.

   (a) Use a repeat loop to write a bisection algorithm to find a root of $f(x) = x^3 + 2x^2 - 7$ to an accuracy of 6 decimal places, given that the root is known to lie between 0 and 2.

   (b) Prove that your bisection algorithm is guaranteed to converge for any continuous function which takes opposite signed values at 0 and 2, and calculate how many loops it will take.

2 We could implement the Sieve of Eratosthenes using a while() loop:

```
> Eratosthenes <- function(n) {
+        # Print prime numbers up to n (based on the sieve of Eratosthenes)
+        if (n >= 2) {
+            sieve <- seq(2, n)
+            primes <- c()
+            while (length(sieve) > 0) {
+                p <- sieve[1]
```

```
+                    primes <- c(primes, p)
+                    sieve <- sieve[(sieve %% p) != 0]
+            }
+            return(primes)
+        } else {
+            stop("Input value of n should be at least 2.")
+        }
+ }
```

(a) Trace through this function until you understand why it works.
(b) Show that once `p >= sqrt(n)` all remaining entries in `sieve` are prime.
(c) Modify this function using `break` to take advantage of the above result.

4.2 | Managing complexity through functions

Most real computer programs are much longer than the examples we give in this book. Most people can't keep the details in their heads all at once, so it is extremely important to find ways to reduce the complexity. There have been any number of different strategies of program design developed over the years. In this section we give a short outline of some of the strategies that have worked for us.

4.2.1 What are functions?

Functions are self-contained units with a well-defined purpose. In general, functions take inputs, do calculations (possibly printing intermediate results, drawing graphs, calling other functions, etc.), and produce outputs. If the inputs and outputs are well-defined, the programmer can be reasonably sure whether the function works or not; and once it works, can move on to the next problem.

Example 4.9
Suppose payments of R dollars are deposited annually into a bank account which earns constant interest i per year. What is the accumulated value of the account at the end of n years, supposing deposits are made at the end of each year?

The total amount at the end of n years is

$$R(1+i)^{n-1} + \cdots + R(1+i) + R = R\frac{(1+i)^n - 1}{i}.$$

An R function to calculate the amount of an annuity is

```
> annuityAmt <- function(n, R, i) {
+     R*((1 + i)^n - 1) / i
+ }
```

If \$400 is deposited annually for 10 years into an account bearing 5% annual interest, we can calculate the accumulated amount using

```
> annuityAmt(10, 400, 0.05)
[1] 5031.157
```

R is somewhat unusual among computer languages in that functions are objects that can be manipulated like other more common objects such as vectors, matrices, and lists.

The definition of a function normally has the following structure:

1 The word `function`.
2 A pair of round parentheses `()` which enclose the argument list. The list may be empty.
3 A single statement, or a sequence of statements enclosed in curly braces `{}`.

Like other R objects, functions are usually named. You should choose the names of your functions to succinctly describe the action of the function. For example, `var()` computes variances, and `median()` computes medians. The name is important: if you choose a name that you can't remember, you will waste time looking it up later. If you choose a name that is misleading about the action of the function (e.g. if we had named our `annuityAmt` function `annuityRate`), you will find your programs extremely hard to understand.

When R executes a function definition, it produces an object with three parts: the header, the body, and a reference to the environment in which the definition was executed.

The first two items in the function definition are used to create the header. The header to an R function describes the inputs, or "arguments." For example, the header of our `Eratosthenes` function above is `function(n)`. This tells us that the function takes one argument named n, which specifies the upper limit for the sieve. The header on `annuityAmt` is `function(n, R, i)`, telling us that it takes three arguments named n, R and i. Functions may take any number of arguments. Again, choose their names to indicate their function.

To reduce the burden on the user of a function, we may give default values to some arguments: if the user doesn't specify the value, the default will be used. For example, we could have used the header

```
annuityAmt <- function(n, R = 1, i = 0.01)
```

to indicate that if a user called `annuityAmt(24)` without specifying R and i, then we should act as though R = 1 and i = 0.01.

The second part of a function is the body. This is a single statement, or sequence of statements in curly braces. They specify what computations are to be carried out by the function. In the original `Eratosthenes` example, the body was

```
{
    if (n >= 2) {
        sieve <- seq(2, n)
        primes <- c()
        for (i in seq(2, n)) {
            if (any(sieve == i)) {
                primes <- c(primes, i)
                sieve <- c(sieve[(sieve %% i) != 0], i)
            }

        }
        return(primes)
    } else {
        stop("Input value of n should be at least 2.")
    }
}
```

At some point in the body of the function there is normally a statement like `return(primes)` which specifies the output value of the function. (In R all functions produce a single output. In some other languages functions may produce no output, or multiple outputs.) If there is no `return()` statement, then the value of the last statement executed is returned. This is how `annuityAmt` returns its value.

The third part of a function is the hardest part to understand, because it is the least concrete: the environment of the function. We won't give a complete description here, but will limit ourselves to the following circular definition: the environment is a reference to the environment in which the function was defined.

What we mean by this is the following. In our `Eratosthenes` function, we made use of two quite different sorts of objects: n, `sieve`, `primes`, and i were all defined locally within the function. There is no ambiguity about what they mean. But `seq`, c, `any`, `return`, and `stop` are not defined there: they were part of the R environment where `Eratosthenes` was defined. (They are all functions, and the local variables were not: this is commonly the case, but it is by no means necessary.)

The really interesting thing is the following. Within the `Eratosthenes` function, we could have defined a new function. *Its* environment would include n, `sieve`, `primes`, and i. For example, we might want to make the removal of multiples of the prime values clearer by putting that operation into a small function called `noMultiples`:

```
> Eratosthenes <- function(n) {
+    # Print all prime numbers up to n (based on the sieve of Eratosthenes)
+       if (n >= 2) {
+
+           noMultiples <- function(j) sieve[(sieve %% j) != 0]
+
```

```
+            sieve <- seq(2, n)
+            primes <- c()
+            for (i in seq(2, n)) {
+                if (any(sieve == i)) {
+                    primes <- c(primes, i)
+                    sieve <-c(noMultiples(i), i)
+                }
+            }
+            return(primes)
+        } else {
+            stop("Input value of n should be at least 2.")
+        }
+ }
```

The noMultiples function defines j in its header, so j is a local variable, and it finds sieve in its environment.

Exercises

1 Verify that the objects var, cos, median, read.table, and dump are all functions.[4]

2 Suppose Mr. Ng deposits a certain amount (say, P) of money in a bank where the interest rate is i.r, and interest is compounded. If he leaves the money in the bank for n interest conversion periods, it will accumulate to

$$P(1 + i.r)^n.$$

(a) Write an R function called compound.interest() which computes this amount. Your function should have three arguments.
(b) Often, one interest conversion period is equal to 1 month. In this case, how much will Mr. Ng have in the bank at the end of 30 months, if he deposits $1000, and the interest rate is 1% per month?

3 Write a function which uses the bisection algorithm to calculate the zero of a user-supplied function.

4.2.2 Scope of variables

The "scope" of a variable tells us where the variable would be recognized. For example, variables defined within functions have local scope, so they are only recognized within the function. A variable could be created with the same name in a different function but there is no risk of a clash.

Example 4.10

In this example we create two functions f and g, both with local variables named x. g is called by f and modifies its instance of x without affecting the x in f.

```
> f <- function() {
+     x <- 1
+     g()   # g will have no effect on our local x
+     return(x)
+ }
```

[4] It is conventional to refer to functions with parentheses after the name, i.e. as var(), cos(), etc. We didn't do that here in order to avoid the ambiguity: do we mean the var object, or the result returned by a call to var()?

```
> g <- function() {
+    x <- 2     # this changes g's local x, not the one in f
+ }
> f()
[1] 1
```

In R, scope is controlled by the environment of functions. Variables defined at the console have global scope, meaning they are visible in any user-defined function. Variables defined in a function are visible in the function, and in functions defined within it.

Using local variables rather than globals helps tremendously in programming, because while you are writing the function, you don't need to worry about some other part of the program changing the values of your variables. You can predict their values from the code you write, and be sure that once you get it correct, you can trust it.

R also has "packages," which are collections of functions and data. Normally packages have their own scope (known as their "namespace"), but the details of namespaces (and of packages without namespaces) are beyond the scope of this text.

4.3 | Miscellaneous programming tips

4.3.1   Using `fix()`

Sometimes we make errors when we write functions. To help us replace the incorrect version with a new one, the `fix()` function can be used to make corrections. `fix()` can also be used to create functions.

Example 4.11
Type `fix(Eratosthenes)` to make changes to the `Eratosthenes` function.

Example 4.12
Type `fix(factorial)` to create a template for a new function named `factorial`. The argument and body are ready to be filled in.

To create an object that computes factorials, we will use the `prod()` function. This function multiplies all of the elements in its argument together. Therefore,

```
prod(1:n)
```

should produce $n!$. The above statement belongs in the body (between the curly brackets), while the header will be `function(n)`.

Exit from the editor, and experiment with the new `factorial()` function.

4.3.2 Documentation using

The # symbol is a simple way of inserting comments such as titles and descriptions into R functions and scripts. R ignores all text from the # character to the end of the line.

It is good practice to add a title and short description to any function that you create, so that you and other users can be reminded later of the purpose of the function. It is surprising how easy it is to forget the purpose of a function created only a few weeks or months ago.

It is also sometimes useful to describe what a particular line of code does. This is especially useful when an obscure command has been used.

Exercises

1 Compute 10!, 50!, 100!, and 1000!

2 (a) Using `fix()` and `factorial()`, create a function which computes the binomial coefficient

$$\binom{n}{m}.$$

(b) Compute $\binom{4}{2}$, $\binom{50}{20}$, and $\binom{5000}{2000}$.

(c) The `sum()` function can be used to sum up all elements of its argument, while the `log()` and `exp()` functions take the natural logarithm and exponential of all elements in their argument. Use these functions to create an improved function to compute binomial coefficients.

(d) Compute $\binom{4}{2}$, $\binom{50}{20}$, and $\binom{5000}{2000}$ using the improved version.

3 Refer to Exercise 2 of Section 4.2.1 in which you created a function called `compound.interest()`. Often, the interest rate is quoted as a nominal annual rate, compounded monthly. To obtain the monthly rate, the nominal annual rate is simply divided by 12. More generally, if there are m interest conversion periods in a year, the nominal annual rate is divided by m to obtain the effective interest rate for the appropriate conversion period (e.g. if the compounding is daily, the nominal annual rate is divided by 365). Fix `compound.interest()` so that a nominal annual interest rate j and m, the number of conversion periods per year are part of the argument. The effective rate $i.r$ is assigned j/m in the body of the function. (You may delete $i.r$ from the argument list.)

4 Use the new `compound.interest()` function to compute the amount accumulated from $1000 at an annual rate of 12%, compounded daily. Compare this with the amount accumulated if the compounding is monthly or yearly.

5 Suppose Ms. Wu wishes to take out a mortgage on a house. She wants to know what her periodic payments will be. If P is the initial amount mortgaged, $i.r$ is the effective interest rate, and n is the length of the mortgage, then the periodic payment R is given by

$$R = \frac{Pi.r}{1 - (1 + i.r)^{-n}}.$$

(a) Construct a function called `mortgage.payment()` which employs this formula.

(b) Calculate Ms. Wu's monthly payments, if the initial amount is $100 000, the interest rate is 1% and the number of interest conversion periods is 300.

(c) Use the `annuity()` function to compute accumulated amounts after 10 years, with periodic payments of $400, but with a vector of interest rates ranging from 0.01 through 0.20, by increments of 0.01.

4.4 Some general programming guidelines

Writing a computer program to solve a problem can usually be reduced to following this sequence of steps:

1 Understand the problem.
2 Work out a general idea how to solve it.
3 Translate your general idea into a detailed implementation.
4 Check: Does it work?
  Is it good enough?
  If yes, you are done!
  If no, go back to step 2.

Example 4.13
We wish to write a program which will sort a vector of integers into increasing order.

1 Understand the problem. A good way to understand your programming problem is to try a specific case. You will often need to consider a simple case, but take care not to make it too trivial. For the sorting problem, we might consider sorting the vector consisting of the elements $3, 5, 24, 6, 2, 4, 13, 1$.
We will write a function to be called `sort()` for which we could do the following:

```
x <- c(3, 5, 24, ..., 1)
sort(x)
```

The output should be the numbers in increasing order: $1, 2, 3, 4, 5, 6, 13, 24$.

2 Work out a general idea. A first idea might be to find where the smallest value is, and put it aside. Then repeat, with the remaining values, setting aside the smallest value each time.
An alternative idea: compare successive pairs of values, starting at the beginning of the vector, and running through to the end. Swap pairs if they are out of order.
After checking, you will find that the alternative idea doesn't work. Try using this idea on $2, 1, 4, 3, 0$, for example. After running through it, you should end up with $1, 2, 3, 0, 4$.

In your check of this alternate idea, you may notice that the largest value always lands at the end of the new vector. (Can you prove to yourself that this should always happen?) This means that we can sort the vector by starting at the beginning of the vector, and going through all adjacent pairs. Then repeat this procedure for all but the last value, and so on.

3 Detailed implementation. At the implementation stage, we need to address specific coding questions. In this sorting problem, one question to be addressed is: How do we swap x[i] *and* x[i+1]?
Here is a way to swap the value of x[3] with that of x[4]:

```
> save <- x[3]
> x[3] <- x[4]
> x[4] <- save
```

Note that you should not over-write the value of x[3] with the value of x[4] before its old value has been saved in another place; otherwise, you will not be able to assign that value to x[4].
We are now ready to write the code:

```
> sort <- function(x) {
+       # x is initially the input vector and will be modified to form
+       # the output
+       # first is compared with last
+       for(last in length(x):2){
+           for(first in 1:(last-1)) {
+               if(x[first] > x[first + 1]) {      # swap the pair
+                   save <- x[first]
+                   x[first] <- x[first + 1]
+                   x[first + 1] <- save
+               }
+           }
+       }
+       return (x)
+ }
```

4 Check. Always begin testing your code on simple examples to identify obvious bugs:

```
> sort(c(2, 1))
[1] 1 2
> sort(c(2, 24, 3, 4, 5, 13, 6, 1))
[1]  1  2  3  4  5  6 13 24
```

Try the code on several other numeric vectors. What is the output when the input vector has length 1?

```
> sort(1)
Error in if (x[first] > x[first + 1]) {: missing value where
TRUE/FALSE needed
```

The problem here is that when `length(x) == 1`, the value of `last` will take on the values `1:2`, rather than no values at all. This doesn't require a redesign of the function, we can fix it by handling this as a special case at the beginning of our function:

```
> sort <- function(x) {
+        # x is initially the input vector and will be modified to form
+        # the output
+
+        if (length(x) < 2) return (x)
+
+        # last is the last element to compare with
+
+        for(last in length(x):2) {
+            for(first in 1:(last - 1)) {
+                if(x[first] > x[first + 1]) {      # swap the pair
+                    save <- x[first]
+                    x[first] <- x[first + 1]
+                    x[first + 1] <- save
+                }
+            }
+        }
+        return (x)
+ }
```

Test the new version:

```
> sort(1)
[1] 1
```

Success! (Or at least we hope so. Have we missed anything?)

4.4.1 Top-down design

Working out the detailed implementation of a program can appear to be a daunting task. The key to making it manageable is to break it down into smaller pieces which you know how to solve. One strategy for doing that is known as "top-down design." Top-down design is similar to outlining an essay before filling in the details:

1 Write out the whole program in a small number (1–5) of steps.
2 Expand each step into a small number of steps.
3 Keep going until you have a program.

Example 4.14
The sort algorithm described in Example 4.13 is known as a "bubble sort." The bubble sort is easy to program and is efficient when the vector x is short, but when x is longer, more efficient methods are available. One of these is known as a "merge sort."

The general idea of a merge sort is to split the vector into two halves, sort each half, and then merge the two halves. During the merge, we only need to compare the first elements of each sorted half to decide which is the smallest value over all. Remove that value from its half; then the second value becomes the smallest remaining value in this half, and we can proceed to put the two parts together into one sorted vector.

So how do we do the initial sorting of each half? We could use a bubble sort, but a more elegant procedure is to use a merge sort on each of them. This is an idea called *recursion*. The `mergesort()` function which we will write below can make calls to itself. Because of variable scoping, new copies of all of the local variables will be created each time it is called, and the different calls will not interfere with each other.

Understanding the idea

It is often worthwhile to consider small numerical examples in order to ensure that we understand the basic idea of the algorithm, before we proceed to designing it in detail. For example, suppose x is [8, 6, 7, 4], and we want to construct a sorted result r. Then our merge sort would proceed as follows:

1 Split x into two parts: $y \leftarrow [8, 6]$, $z \leftarrow [7, 4]$.
2 Sort y and z: $y \leftarrow [6, 8]$, $z \leftarrow [4, 7]$.
3 Merge y and z:
    (a) Compare $y_1 = 6$ and $z_1 = 4$: $r_1 \leftarrow 4$; remove z_1; z is now [7].
    (b) Compare $y_1 = 6$ and $z_1 = 7$: $r_2 \leftarrow 6$; remove y_1; y is now [8].
    (c) Compare $y_1 = 8$ and $z_1 = 7$: $r_3 \leftarrow 7$; remove z_1; z is now empty.
    (d) Append remaining values of y onto r: $r_4 \leftarrow 8$.
4 Return $r = [4, 6, 7, 8]$.

Translating into code

It is helpful to think of the translation process as a stepwise process of refining a program until it works.

We begin with a general statement, and gradually expand each part. We will use a double comment marker `##` to mark descriptive lines that still need expansion. We will number these comments so that we can refer to them in the text; in practice, you would probably not find this necessary. After expanding, we will change to the usual comment marker to leave our description in place.

We start with just one aim, which we can use as our first descriptive line:

```
## 1.   Use a merge sort to sort a vector
```

We will slowly expand upon previous steps, adding in detail as we go. A simple expansion of step 1 follows from recognizing that we need an input vector x which will be processed by a function that we are naming `mergesort`. Somehow, we will sort this vector. In the end, we want the output to be returned:

```
# 1.   Use a merge sort to sort a vector
mergesort <- function (x) {
    ## 2:     sort x into result
    return (result)
}
```

We now expand step 2, noting how the merge sort algorithm proceeds:

```
# 1.  Use a merge sort to sort a vector
mergesort <- function (x) {
    # 2:      sort x into result
    ## 2.1: split x in half
    ## 2.2: sort each half
    ## 2.3: merge the 2 sorted parts into a sorted result
    return (result)
}
```

Each substep of the above needs to be expanded. First, we expand step 2.1:

```
# 2.1: split x in half
len <- length(x)
x1 <- x[1:(len %/% 2)]
x2 <- x[(len %/% 2 + 1):len]
```

Be careful with "edge" cases; usually, we expect to sort a vector containing more than one element, but our sort function should be able to handle the simple problem of sorting a single element. The code above does not handle len < 2 properly.

We must try again, fixing step 2.1. The solution is simple: if the length of x is 0 or 1, our function should simply return x. Otherwise, we proceed to split x and sort as above. This affects code outside of step 2.1, so we need to correct our outline. Here is the new outline, including the new step 2.1:

```
# 1.  Use a merge sort to sort a vector
mergesort <- function (x) {
    # Check for a vector that doesn't need sorting
    len <- length(x)
    if (len < 2) result  <- x
    else {
        # 2: sort x into result
        # 2.1: split x in half
        y <- x[1:(len %/% 2)]
        z <- x[(len %/% 2 + 1):len]
        ## 2.2: sort y and z
        ## 2.3: merge y and z into a sorted result
    }
    return(result)
}
```

Step 2.2 is very easy to expand, because we can make use of our mergesort() function, even though we haven't written it yet! The key idea is to remember that we are not executing the code at this point, we are designing it. We should assume our design will eventually be successful, and we will be able to make use of the fruits of our labour. So step 2.2 becomes

```
# 2.2: sort y and z
y <- mergesort(y)
z <- mergesort(z)
```

Step 2.3 is more complicated, so let's take it slowly. We know that we will need a `result` vector, but let's describe the rest of the process before we code it. We repeat the whole function here, including this expansion and the expansion of step 2.2:

```
# 1.  Use a merge sort to sort a vector
mergesort <- function (x) {
    # Check for a vector that doesn't need sorting
    len <- length(x)
    if (len < 2) result   <- x
    else {
        # 2: sort x into result
        # 2.1: split x in half
        y <- x[1:(len %/% 2)]
        z <- x[(len %/% 2 + 1):len]
        # 2.2: sort y and z
        y <- mergesort(y)
        z <- mergesort(z)
        # 2.3: merge y and z into a sorted result
        result <- c()
        ## 2.3.1:   while (some are left in both piles)
        ## 2.3.2:       put the smallest first element on the end
        ## 2.3.3:       remove it from y or z
        ## 2.3.4:   put the leftovers onto the end of result
    }
    return(result)
}
```

The final steps are now easy to expand. Steps 2.3.2 and 2.3.3 end up intertwined, because they both depend on the test of which of `y[1]` and `z[1]` is smallest.

```
> # 1.  Use a merge sort to sort a vector
> mergesort <- function (x) {
+     # Check for a vector that doesn't need sorting
+     len <-length(x)
+     if (len < 2) result   <- x
+     else {
+         # 2: sort x into result
+         # 2.1: split x in half
+         y <- x[1:(len %/% 2)]
+         z <- x[(len %/% 2 + 1):len]
+         # 2.2: sort y and z
+         y <- mergesort(y)
+         z <- mergesort(z)
+         # 2.3: merge y and z into a sorted result
+         result <- c()
+         # 2.3.1:   while (some are left in both piles)
+         while (min(length(y), length(z)) > 0) {
```

```
+                # 2.3.2:        put the smallest first element on the end
+                # 2.3.3:        remove it from y or z
+                if (y[1] < z[1]) {
+                     result <- c(result, y[1])
+                     y <- y[-1]
+                } else {
+                      result <- c(result, z[1])
+                      z <- z[-1]
+                }
+           }
+           # 2.3.4:    put the leftovers onto the end of result
+      if (length(y) > 0)
+                result <- c(result, y)
+      else
+                result <- c(result, z)
+      }
+           return(result)
+ }
```

Exercises

1 Modify the mergesort function described in this section so that it takes a logical argument (called decreasing) which causes sorting in decreasing order when set to TRUE.
2 The equations

$$f(x, y) = 0$$
$$g(x, y) = 0 \tag{4.2}$$

can be solved numerically using a form of Newton's method. Assign initial guesses to each of x_0 and y_0.
Then perform the following iteration, for $n = 1, 2, \ldots$:

$$x_n = x_{n-1} - (g_{y,n-1}f_{n-1} - f_{y,n-1}g_{n-1})/d_{n-1}$$

$$y_n = y_{n-1} - (f_{x,n-1}g_{n-1} - g_{x,n-1}f_{n-1})/d_{n-1},$$

where

$$f_{x,n-1} = \frac{\partial f}{\partial x}(x_{n-1}, y_{n-1})$$

$$f_{y,n-1} = \frac{\partial f}{\partial y}(x_{n-1}, y_{n-1})$$

$$g_{x,n-1} = \frac{\partial g}{\partial x}(x_{n-1}, y_{n-1})$$

$$g_{y,n-1} = \frac{\partial g}{\partial y}(x_{n-1}, y_{n-1})$$

$$f_{n-1} = f(x_{n-1}, y_{n-1})$$

$$g_{n-1} = g(x_{n-1}, y_{n-1}),$$

and

$$d_{n-1} = f_{x,n-1}g_{y,n-1} - f_{y,n-1}g_{x,n-1}.$$

The iteration is terminated when the function values are close enough to 0.

(a) Write a function which will perform this iteration.
(b) Apply the function to the system

$$\begin{aligned}
x + y &= 0 \\
x^2 + 2y^2 - 2 &= 0.
\end{aligned}$$

Find the two solutions to this system analytically as a check on your numerical result.

4.5 | Debugging and maintenance

Computer errors are called "bugs." Removing these errors from a program is called "debugging." Debugging is difficult, and one of our goals is to write programs that don't have bugs in them: but sometimes we make mistakes.

We have found that the following five steps help us to find and fix bugs in our own programs:

1 Recognize that a bug exists.
2 Make the bug reproducible.
3 Identify the cause of the bug.
4 Fix the error and test.
5 Look for similar errors.

We will consider each of these in turn.

4.5.1 Recognizing that a bug exists

Sometimes this is easy; if the program doesn't work, there is a bug. However, in other cases the program seems to work, but the output is incorrect, or the program works for some inputs, but not for others. A bug causing this kind of error is much more difficult to recognize.

There are several strategies to make it easier. First, follow the advice in previous sections of this text, and break up your program into simple, self-contained functions. Document their inputs and outputs. Within the function, test that the inputs obey your assumptions about them, and think of test inputs where you can see at a glance whether the outputs match your expectations.

In some situations, it may be worthwhile writing *two* versions of a function: one that may be too slow to use in practice, but which you are sure is right, and another that is faster but harder to be sure about. Test that both versions produce the same output in all situations.

When errors only occur for certain inputs, our experience shows that those are often what are called "edge cases": situations which are right on the boundary between legal and illegal inputs. Test those! For example, test what happens when you try a vector of length zero, test very large or very small values, etc.

4.5.2   Make the bug reproducible

Before you can fix a bug, you need to know where things are going wrong. This is *much* easier if you know how to trigger the bug. Bugs that only appear unpredictably are extremely difficult to fix. The good news is that for the most part computers are predictable: if you give them the same inputs, they give you the same outputs. The difficulty is in working out what the necessary inputs are.

For example, a common mistake in programming is to misspell the name of a variable. Normally this results in an immediate error message, but sometimes you accidentally choose a variable that actually does exist. Then you'll probably get the wrong answer, and the answer you get may appear to be random, because it depends on the value in some unrelated variable.

The key to tracking down this sort of problem is to work hard to make the error reproducible. Simplify things as much as possible: start a new empty R session, and see if you can reproduce it. Once you can reproduce the error, you will eventually be able to track it down.

Some programs do random simulations. For those, you can make the simulations reproducible by setting the value of the random number seed (see Chapter 5) at the start.

4.5.3   Identify the cause of the bug

When you have confirmed that a bug exists, the next step is to identify its cause. If your program has stopped with an error, read the error messages. Try to understand them as well as you can.

In R, you can obtain extra information about an error message using the `traceback()` function. When an error occurs, R saves information about the current stack of active functions, and `traceback()` prints this list.

Example 4.15
In this function we calculate the coefficient of variation as the standard deviation of a variable, after dividing by its mean. However, the coefficient of variation of the value 0 gives an error.

```
> cv <- function(x) {
+     sd(x / mean(x))
+ }
> cv(0)
Error in var(x, na.rm = na.rm) : missing observations in cov/cor
```

The error message talks about the function `var()`, which we didn't use. To find out where it was called from, we use `traceback()`:

```
> traceback()
3: var(x, na.rm = na.rm)
2: sd(x/mean(x))
1: cv(0)
```

This shows that the standard function `sd()` calls `var()`, and that's where the error was found. Our calculation of `x/mean(x)` must have given a missing value. When we try this calculation directly, we see why:

```
> x <- 0
> mean(x)
[1] 0
> x / mean(x)
[1] NaN
```

The solution to this is to check the input on entry to our `cv()` function. The standard definition of the coefficient of variation requires all x values to be positive, so we'll check for that before doing the calculation:

```
> cv <- function(x) {
+       stopifnot(all(x > 0))
+       sd(x / mean(x))
+ }
> cv(0)
Error: all(x > 0) is not TRUE
```

We use the standard function `stopifnot()` to stop execution when the condition `all(x > 0)` is not TRUE.

The `traceback()` function shows *where* an error is happening, but it doesn't show *why*. Furthermore, many bugs don't trigger any error message, you just see that your program is giving the wrong answer.

How do you work out what is going wrong?

With proper planning beforehand, this step can be made somewhat easier. The advice above in Section 4.5.1 also helps here. If you have chosen meaningful names for variables, you can check whether they contain what you think they contain by printing their values. The simplest way to do this is to edit your functions to add statements like this:

```
cat("In cv, x=", x, "\n")
```

This will print the value of x, identifying where the message is coming from. The `"\n"` at the end tells R to go to a new line after printing. You may want to use `print()` rather than `cat()` to take advantage of its formatting, but remember that it can only print one thing at a time, so you would likely use it as

```
cat("In cv, x=\n")
print(x)
```

A more flexible way to examine the values in functions is to use the `browser()` or `debug()` or functions discussed in Section 4.5.6.

Another great way to understand what is going wrong in a small function is to simulate it by hand. Act as you think R would act, and write down the values of all variables as the function progresses. In combination with the techniques described above, this can also identify misconceptions about R: if your simulation would print different results than the real R prints, then you've identified a possible cause of your bug: R is not behaving as you expect. Most likely this is because you don't know R well enough yet, but it is possible that you have actually discovered a bug in R!

4.5.4 Fixing errors and testing

Once you have identified the bug in your program, you need to fix it. Try to fix it in such a way that you don't cause a different problem. Then test what you've done! You should put together tests that include the way you know that would reproduce the error, as well as edge cases, and anything else you can think of.

4.5.5 Look for similar errors elsewhere

Often when you have found and fixed a bug, you can recognize the kind of mistake you made. It is worthwhile looking through the rest of your program for similar errors, because if you made the mistake once, you may have made it twice.

4.5.6 The `browser()` and `debug()` functions

Rather than using `cat()` or `print()` for debugging, R allows you to call the function `browser()`. This will pause execution of your function, and allow you to examine (or change!) local variables, or execute any other R command, inside the evaluation environment of the function.

You can also execute a debugger command:

- n – "next"; execute the next line of code, single-stepping through the function
- c – "continue"; let the function continue running
- Q – quit the debugger.

Another way to enter the browser is to use the `debug()` function. You mark function `f` for debugging using `debug(f)`, and then the browser will be called when you enter the function. Turn off debugging using `undebug(f)`.

Example 4.16
Consider the `mergesort()` function constructed earlier. We will apply the `debug()` function and check the value of the x argument before any other calculation is completed, and then the values of y and z just before sorting them.

```
> debug(mergesort)        # Set the debugging flag on mergesort
> mergesort(c(3, 5, 4, 2))  # This stops and displays the function
debugging in: mergesort(c(3, 5, 4, 2))
debug: {
    len <- length(x)
    if (len < 2)
        result <- x
```

```
    else {
        y <- x[1:(len / 2)]
        z <- x[(len / 2 + 1):len]
        y <- mergesort(y)
        z <- mergesort(z)
        result <- c()
        while (min(length(y), length(z)) > 0) {
            if (y[1] < z[1]) {
                result <- c(result, y[1])
                y <- y[-1]
            }
            else {
                result <- c(result, z[1])
                z <- z[-1]
            }
        }
        if (length(y) > 0)
            result <- c(result, y)
        else result <- c(result, z)
    }
    return(result)
}
Browse[1]> x     # This shows the value of x on entry
[1] 3 5 4 2
Browse[1]> n     # Enter the body
debug: len <- length(x)
 Browse[1]>      # Enter is the same as n: execute the
assignment to len
debug: if (len < 2) result <- x else {
    y <- x[1:(len / 2)]
    z <- x[(len / 2 + 1):len]
    ...          # The if statement is shown, but we have deleted it
Browse[1]> n
debug: y <- x[1:(len / 2)]
Browse[1]> n
debug: z <- x[(len / 2 + 1):len]
Browse[1]> n
debug: y <- mergesort(y)
Browse[1]> y     # Look at y just before the call to
mergesort
[1] 3 5
Browse[1]> z     # Look at z
[1] 4 2
Browse[1]> Q     # Hitting enter again would enter the mergesort that
                 # sorts y
                 # We use Q to quit instead
> undebug(mergesort)  # Remove the debug marker from mergesort
```

4.6 | Efficient programming

When producing computer code, you may find that it runs slower than you want it to, even on today's fast computers. But take heart: there are always ways to speed up a program. The process is called *optimization*. In this section we will give a few examples of *hand optimization* in R: ways to rewrite your code so that it runs faster. Other possibilities are automatic optimization (not available in R, but some other programming platforms can do this), or hardware optimization, where you change your computer to run your programs faster, e.g. by buying a new one.

Optimization always requires some sort of trade-off. Hand optimization can be time consuming, and since optimized code can be harder to understand, errors can slip by undetected. You should always ensure that your code is correct before you try to optimize it because it will probably be harder to debug later. You should use judgment about whether optimization will be worthwhile.

4.6.1 Learn your tools

In order to write efficient code, you need to understand the platform you are working with. For example, R is designed to work with vectors. Operations on whole vectors are usually much faster than working one element at a time. Summing two vectors could be done as follows:

```
> X <- rnorm(100000)      # Xi ~ N(0, 1) i=1, ..., 100 000
> Y <- rnorm(100000)      # Yi ~ N(0, 1) i=1, ..., 100 000
> Z <- c()
> for (i in 1:100000) {
+     Z <- c(Z, X[i] + Y[i])   #  this takes about 53 seconds
+ }
```

However, this is extremely inefficient in R. First, it reallocates the vector Z 100 000 times, increasing its length by one each time. Since we know the length of Z in advance, we could allocate it once, and modify its entries:

```
> Z <- rep(NA, 100000)
> for (i in 1:100000) {
+     Z[i] <- X[i] + Y[i]      #  this takes about 0.88 seconds
+ }
```

Simply by avoiding the reallocations, we have speeded up the operation by a factor of approximately 60 times.

A more natural way to do this calculation in R is by vectorizing completely, i.e.

```
> Z <- X + Y                   #    0.002 seconds (approx)
```

The fully vectorized calculation is another 440 times faster, i.e. 26 500 times faster than the original loop. If the original code had taken a year to run, the optimized code would be done in about 20 minutes, making the difference between an infeasible solution and a feasible one.

However, the original code in our example took 53 seconds to run, and the optimized version 2 milliseconds: an impressive ratio, but still only a savings of 53 seconds. In this case the revised code is clearer and more obvious than the original so we think the effort was worthwhile. But if we had been forced to spend a lot of time on the optimization, and had ended up with obscure code that we wouldn't understand the next time we looked at it, we would judge the effort not to have been worth it.

4.6.2 Use efficient algorithms

Example 4.17
Think about the problem of recording grades in a spreadsheet. You have a pile of tests from a class. There are n tests, each with a name and grade. You also have a class list in a spreadsheet, and want to record the grades there.

A really slow algorithm
1 Read the name of the first student in the mark spreadsheet.
2 Randomly select one of the n tests.
3 If the names match, record the grade, and go on to the next student.
4 If not, put the test back, and randomly select another.
5 Continue until all grades have been recorded.

How bad is this algorithm? One answer to this question is to determine the expected time until we get our first matching grade.

Since there are n tests, the probability of a correct match is $1/n$. The number of draws until the first match is a geometric random variable with parameter $1/n$. The expected value for that random variable is known to be n. When we get to the second student, the expected value will be $n - 1$, because there is one less test to search. Overall, the expected time to completely record all of the grades is $\sum_{i=1}^{n} i = n(n-1)/2$ times the amount of time to do one selection and check.

A slightly faster algorithm
1 Take the first test.
2 Scan through all the names in the spreadsheet until you find the matching name, and record the grade.
3 Repeat for each student.

For each test, this algorithm requires scanning an average of half the names in the list, so the total time is $n^2/2$ times the time to scan one name, plus n times the time to select a test from the pile. Even though this is a total of $n^2/2 + n = n(n+2)/2$ steps, each step is faster than the steps above, so this algorithm is probably faster.

A much faster algorithm
1 First, sort the names in the spreadsheet into alphabetical order.
2 Take the first test.
3 Search for the name in the spreadsheet, using the alphabetical sorting to help.
4 Repeat for each student.

This is much faster, because searching through a sorted list can be quicker, using a bisection technique: check the middle name, then the middle name of whichever half the current test falls in, and so on. Each test takes about $\log_2 n$ comparisons before you'll find it, so the whole operation takes $n \log_2 n$ operations. For a medium to large class this is much better than the $n^2/2$ lookup time of the previous algorithm. For a class of 100, it's the difference between 5 000 operations and fewer than 700.

We could go further, and sort the tests before recording them: since the tests and the class list will be in the same order, the recording would take just n steps. However, the sorting of the tests is probably much slower than sorting the names in the spreadsheet, since it requires physical sorting rather than just asking the computer to sort the names, so this will likely be slower than the algorithm above. On the other hand, it leaves the tests in sorted order so other future operations on them (e.g. looking up the test of a particular student) would be faster. It will require a judgment whether the additional investment now will pay off in saved time later.

4.6.3 Measure the time your program takes

Optimization is hard work, so you don't want to do it when it's not necessary. In many cases, it will take more time to optimize a program than you could ever hope to save from the optimization. Before starting to optimize, you should measure the amount of time your program is taking, as an upper bound on the amount of time you could possibly save.

In R, the `system.time()` function measures the execution time of evaluating expressions. For example,

```
> X <- rnorm(100000)
> Y <- rnorm(100000)
> Z <- rep(NA, 100000)
> system.time({
+       for (i in 1:100000) {
+             Z[i] <- X[i] + Y[i]
+       }
+ })

   user   system elapsed
   0.87    0.00    0.88
```

shows how we obtained the timing reported above. The "user" time is the time dedicated to this particular task, the "system" time is how much time your system spent doing other tasks, and the "elapsed" time is the time we would have seen on a clock.

You may also be able to measure which particular parts of your program are the best targets for optimization. A famous rule of thumb in computing is the 90/10 rule: 90% of the execution time of your program comes from 10% of the code. We call code in the slow 10% the *bottlenecks*. The corollary is that if you can identify and optimize the bottlenecks, you can obtain a substantial increase in speed without even looking at 90% of the program.

Many software platforms offer *profilers* to help find the bottlenecks in your program. There are various kinds of profilers, but in general they monitor the program while it is running and report on where the execution time was spent. In R the profiler is controlled by the `Rprof()` function, but a discussion of the details is beyond the scope of this text.

4.6.4 Be willing to use different tools

Much as we love it, we admit that R is not the only computing platform available, and it is not the best tool for all tasks. For raw speed, you are much better off using a compiled language like C, C++, or Fortran. R itself is written in C and Fortran, which is why the operations on vectors go so quickly: most of the work is done in compiled code.

A style of programming that we recommend is to do most of your work in R. In cases where you don't get acceptable speed, identify the bottlenecks, and consider translating those into a compiled language. R has extensive support for linking to code in other languages. Unfortunately this requires a level of technical detail that is again beyond the scope of this book.

4.6.5 Optimize with care

The famous computer scientist Donald Knuth once said, "Premature optimization is the root of all evil (or at least most of it) in programming."[5] We have emphasized above that optimization is difficult and that it is not always advisable. We finish the chapter with this advice for writing efficient code:

1 Get it right.
2 Get it fast enough.
3 Make sure it's still right.

Chapter exercises

1 Write a function which will evaluate polynomials of the form

$$P(x) = c_n x^{n-1} + c_{n-1} x^{n-2} + \cdots + c_2 x + c_1.$$

Your function should take x and the vector of polynomial coefficients as arguments and it should return the value of the evaluated polynomial. Call this function `directpoly()`.

2 Refer to the previous question. For moderate to large values of n, evaluation of a polynomial at x can be done more efficiently using *Horner's Rule*:

(a) Set $a_n \leftarrow c_n$.
(b) For $i = n - 1, \ldots, 1$ set $a_i = a_{i+1} x + c_i$.
(c) Return a_1. (This is the computed value of $P(x)$.)

Write an R function with arguments x and a vector of polynomial coefficients and which returns the value of the polynomial evaluated at x. Call the resulting function `hornerpoly()`. Ensure that your function returns an appropriate vector of values when x is a vector.

5 Knuth, D. E. (1974) Computer programming as art. *Commun. ACM* **17**(12), 671.

3 Do some timings to compare the algorithms used in the previous two questions.

(a) In particular, try the following code:

```
> system.time(directpoly(x=seq(-10, 10, length=5000000),
+                         c(1, -2, 2, 3, 4, 6, 7)))
> system.time(horner(x=seq(-10, 10, length=5000000),
+                      c(1, -2, 2, 3, 4, 6, 7)))
```

(b) What happens to the comparison when the number of polynomial coefficients is smaller? Try the polynomial

$$P(x) = 2x^2 + 17x - 3.$$

4 Using a starting value of 2.9, find the time that it takes for Newton's method to find the zero (to within seven-digit accuracy) of

(a) $(x - 3)e^{-x}$

(b) $(x^2 - 6x + 9)e^{-x}$.

5 Repeat the previous question, using the bisection algorithm and the initial interval $[2.1, 3.1]$.

6 Do a timing comparison of the bubble sort (see Example 4.13) and the merge sort (see Example 4.14). Do the comparison for vectors of length 10, 1000, 10 000, and 100 000. (You may use the function $\texttt{rnorm()}$ to generate vectors for this purpose.)

Simulation

Much of statistics relies on being able to evaluate expectations of random variables, and finding quantiles of distributions.[1] For example:

- In hypothesis testing, the p-value of a sample is defined as the probability of observing data at least as extreme as the sample in hand, given that the null hypothesis is true. This is the expected value of a random variable defined to be 0 when a sample is less extreme, and 1 otherwise.
- The bias of an estimator is defined to be the expected value of the estimator minus the true value that it is estimating.
- Confidence intervals are based on quantiles of the distribution of a pivotal quantity, e.g. $(\bar{X} - \mu)/(s/\sqrt{n})$.

In simple cases we may evaluate these quantities analytically, or use large sample approximations. However, in other cases we need computer-based methods to approximate them.

In this chapter, you will be introduced to Monte Carlo simulation. This introduction will include basic ideas of random (or more properly, *pseudorandom*) number generation. You will then see how to simulate random variables from several of the common probability distributions. Next, we will show you how simulation can be used in a surprising way: to evaluate integrals. The final topics of the chapter on rejection and importance sampling will give you a hint as to what more advanced methods are like.

5.1 Monte Carlo simulation

One of the most general computer-based methods for approximating properties of random variables is the Monte Carlo method.

To approximate the mean $\mu = E(X)$ using the Monte Carlo method, we generate m independent and identically distributed (i.i.d.) copies of X, namely $X_1, \ldots, X_m$, and use the sample mean $\bar{X} = (1/m) \sum X_i$ as an estimate of $E(X)$. For large values of m, $\bar{X}$ gives a good approximation to $E(X)$.[2]

[1] See the Appendix if you need a review of random variables and their properties.

[2] This follows from the law of large numbers.

Furthermore, if m is large the distribution of the sample mean, $\bar{X}$, can be approximated[3] by a normal distribution with mean μ and variance σ^2/m. Here σ^2 is the variance $\text{Var}(X)$, which can be approximated by the sample variance $s^2 = [1/(m-1)]\sum(X_i - \bar{X})^2$. This allows us to construct approximate confidence intervals for μ. For example, $\bar{X} \pm 1.96\,s/\sqrt{m}$ will contain μ approximately 95% of the time.

The remainder of this chapter describes methods for simulating the generation of random variables on a computer. We will describe deterministic methods of generating values, which are then treated as though they are random. It is useful to think of two participants in this process: the programmer hiding behind a curtain knows that the algorithms are deterministic and predictable, but the user of those numbers is unaware of the mechanisms used to compute them, so to that user, the numbers appear random and unpredictable. In practice, both participants may be the same person! To distinguish this scheme from true random numbers which really are unpredictable, we will call our simulated random numbers *pseudorandom numbers* in the remainder of the chapter.

5.2 | Generation of pseudorandom numbers

We begin our discussion of simulation with a brief exploration of the mechanics of pseudorandom number generation. In particular, we will describe one of the simplest methods for simulating independent uniform random variables on the interval [0,1].

A multiplicative congruential random number generator produces a sequence of pseudorandom numbers, $u_0, u_1, u_2, \ldots$, which appear similar to independent uniform random variables on the interval [0,1].

Let m be a large integer, and let b be another integer which is smaller than m. The value of b is often chosen to be near the square root of m. Different values of b and m give rise to pseudorandom number generators of varying quality. There are various criteria available for choosing good values of these parameters, but it is always important to test the resulting generator to ensure that it is providing reasonable results.

To begin, an integer x_0 is chosen between 1 and m. x_0 is called the seed. We discuss strategies for choosing x_0 below.

Once the seed has been chosen, the generator proceeds as follows:

$$x_1 = b\,x_0 \pmod{m}$$
$$u_1 = x_1/m.$$

u_1 is the first pseudorandom number, taking some value between 0 and 1. The second pseudorandom number is then obtained in the same manner:

$$x_2 = b\,x_1 \pmod{m}$$
$$u_2 = x_2/m.$$

u_2 is another pseudorandom number. If m and b are chosen properly and are not disclosed to the user, it is difficult to predict the value of u_2, given the value of u_1 only. In other words, for most practical purposes u_2 is

[3] This is the central limit theorem.

approximately independent of u_1. The method continues according to the following formulas:

$$x_n = b\, x_{n-1} \pmod{m}$$
$$u_n = x_n/m.$$

This method produces numbers which are entirely deterministic, but to an observer who doesn't know the formula above, the numbers *appear* to be random and unpredictable, at least in the short term.

Example 5.1
Take $m = 7$ and $b = 3$. Also, take $x_0 = 2$. Then

$$x_1 = 3 \times 2 \pmod 7 = 6, \quad u_1 = 0.857$$
$$x_2 = 3 \times 6 \pmod 7 = 4, \quad u_2 = 0.571$$
$$x_3 = 3 \times 4 \pmod 7 = 5, \quad u_3 = 0.714$$
$$x_4 = 3 \times 5 \pmod 7 = 1, \quad u_4 = 0.143$$
$$x_5 = 3 \times 1 \pmod 7 = 3, \quad u_5 = 0.429$$
$$x_6 = 3 \times 3 \pmod 7 = 2, \quad u_6 = 0.286.$$

It should be clear that the iteration will set $x_7 = x_1$ and cycle x_i through the same sequence of integers, so the corresponding sequence u_i will also be cyclic. An observer might not easily be able to predict u_2 from u_1, but since $u_{i+6} = u_i$ for all $i > 0$, longer sequences are very easy to predict. In order to produce an unpredictable sequence, it is desirable to have a very large cycle length so that it is unlikely that any observer will ever see a whole cycle. The cycle length cannot be any larger than m, so m would normally be taken to be very large.

Care must be taken in the choice of b and m to ensure that the cycle length is actually m. Note, for example, what happens when $b = 171$ and $m = 29\,241$. Start with $x_0 = 3$, say, then

$$x_1 = 171 \times 3 = 513$$
$$x_2 = 171 \times 513 \pmod{29\,241} = 0.$$

All remaining x_n's will be 0. To avoid this kind of problem, we should choose m so that it is not divisible by b; thus, prime values of m will be preferred. The next example gives a generator with somewhat better behavior.

Example 5.2
The following lines produce 50 pseudorandom numbers based on the multiplicative congruential generator:

$$x_n = 171\, x_{n-1} \pmod{30\,269}$$
$$u_n = x_n/30\,269,$$

with initial seed $x_0 = 27\,218$.

```
> random.number <- numeric(50)  # this will store the
>                               # pseudorandom output
> random.seed <- 27218
> for (j in 1:50) {
+       random.seed <- (171 * random.seed) %% 30269
+       random.number[j] <- random.seed / 30269
+ }
```

The results, stored in the vector random.number, are as follows. Note that the vector elements range between 0 and 1. These are the pseudorandom numbers, $u_1, u_2, \ldots, u_{50}$.

```
> random.number
 [1]  0.76385080 0.61848756 0.76137302 0.19478675 0.30853348 0.75922561
 [7]  0.82757937 0.51607255 0.24840596 0.47741914 0.63867323 0.21312234
[13]  0.44391952 0.91023820 0.65073177 0.27513297 0.04773861 0.16330239
[19]  0.92470845 0.12514454 0.39971588 0.35141564 0.09207440 0.74472232
[25]  0.34751726 0.42545178 0.75225478 0.63556774 0.68208398 0.63636063
[31]  0.81766824 0.82126929 0.43704780 0.73517460 0.71485678 0.24051009
[37]  0.12722587 0.75562457 0.21180085 0.21794575 0.26872378 0.95176583
[43]  0.75195745 0.58472364 0.98774324 0.90409330 0.59995375 0.59209092
[49]  0.24754700 0.33053619
```

A similar kind of operation (though using a different formula, and with a *much* longer cycle) is used internally by R to produce pseudorandom numbers automatically with the function runif().

Syntax
```
runif(n, min = a, max = b)
```

Execution of this command produces n pseudorandom uniform numbers on the interval $[a, b]$. The default values are $a = 0$ and $b = 1$. The seed is selected internally.

Example 5.3
Generate five uniform pseudorandom numbers on the interval $[0, 1]$, and 10 uniform such numbers on the interval $[-3, -1]$.

```
> runif(5)
[1] 0.9502223 0.3357378 0.1330718 0.4901114 0.0607455
> runif(10, min = -3, max = -1)
 [1] -2.284105 -2.545768 -2.199852 -1.126908 -1.324746 -2.744848
 [7] -1.549739 -1.445740 -2.834744 -1.372574
```

If you execute the above code yourself, you will almost certainly obtain different results than those displayed in our output. This is because the starting seed that you will use will be different from the one that was selected when we ran our code.

There are two different strategies for choosing the starting seed x_0. If the goal is to make an unpredictable sequence, then a random value is desirable. For example, the computer might determine the current time of day to the nearest millisecond, then base the starting seed on the number of milliseconds past the start of the minute. To avoid predictability, this external randomization should only be done once, after which the formula above should be used for updates. For example, if the computer clock were used as above before generating *every* u_i, on a fast computer there would be long sequences of identical values that were generated within a millisecond of each other.

The second strategy for choosing x_0 is to use a fixed, non-random value, e.g. $x_0 = 1$. This makes the sequence of u_i values predictable and repeatable. This would be useful when debugging a program that uses random numbers, or in other situations where repeatability is needed. The way to do this in R is to use the set.seed() function.

For example,

```
> set.seed(32789)   # this ensures that your output will match ours
> runif(5)
[1] 0.3575211 0.3537589 0.2672321 0.9969302 0.1317401
```

Exercises

1 Generate 20 pseudorandom numbers using

$$x_n = 172\, x_{n-1} \pmod{30\,307},$$

with initial seed $x_0 = 17\,218$.

2 Generate 20 pseudorandom numbers using the multiplicative congruential generator with $b = 171$ and $m = 32\,767$ with an initial seed of 2018.

3 Use the runif() function (with set.seed(32078)) to generate 10 pseudorandom numbers from
   (a) the uniform $(0, 1)$ distribution
   (b) the uniform $(3, 7)$ distribution
   (c) the uniform $(-2, 2)$ distribution.

4 Generate 1000 uniform pseudorandom variates using the runif() function, assigning them to a vector called U. Use set.seed(19908).

   (a) Compute the average, variance, and standard deviation of the numbers in U.
   (b) Compare your results with the true mean, variance, and standard deviation.
   (c) Compute the proportion of the values of U that are less than 0.6, and compare with the probability that a uniform random variable U is less than 0.6.
   (d) Estimate the expected value of $1/(U + 1)$.
   (e) Construct a histogram of the values of U, and of 1/(U+1).

5 Simulate 10 000 independent observations on a uniformly distributed random variable on the interval [3.7, 5.8].

(a) Estimate the mean, variance, and standard deviation of such a uniform random variable and compare your estimates with the true values.

(b) Estimate the probability that such a random variable is greater than 4.0. Compare with the true value.

6 Simulate 10 000 values of a uniform $(0, 1)$ random variable, U_1, using `runif()`, and simulate another set of 10 000 values of a uniform $(0, 1)$ random variable U_2. Assign these vectors to `U1` and `U2`, respectively. Since the values in `U1` and `U2` are approximately independent, we can view U_1 and U_2 as independent uniform $(0, 1)$ random variables.

(a) Estimate $E[U_1 + U_2]$. Compare with the true value, and compare with an estimate of $E[U_1] + E[U_2]$.

(b) Estimate $\text{Var}(U_1 + U_2)$ and $\text{Var}(U_1) + \text{Var}(U_2)$. Are they equal? Should the true values be equal?

(c) Estimate $P(U_1 + U_2 \leq 1.5)$.

(d) Estimate $P(\sqrt{U_1} + \sqrt{U_2}) \leq 1.5)$.

7 Suppose U_1, U_2 and U_3 are independent uniform random variables on the interval $(0, 1)$. Use simulation to estimate the following quantities:

(a) $E[U_1 + U_2 + U_3]$

(b) $\text{Var}(U_1 + U_2 + U_3)$ and $\text{Var}(U_1) + \text{Var}(U_2) + \text{Var}(U_3)$

(c) $E\left[\sqrt{U_1 + U_2 + U_3}\right]$

(d) $P\left(\sqrt{U_1} + \sqrt{U_2} + \sqrt{U_3} \geq 0.8\right)$.

8 Use the `round()` function together with `runif()` to generate 1000 pseudorandom integers which take values from 1 through 10, assigning these values to a vector called `discreteunif`. Use the `table()` function to check whether the observed frequencies for each value are close to what you expect. If they are not close, how should you modify your procedure?

9 The `sample()` function allows you to take a simple random sample from a vector of values. For example,

```
sample(c(3,5,7),size = 2, replace = FALSE)
```

will yield a vector of two values taken (without replacement) from the set $\{3, 5, 7\}$. Use the `sample()` function to generate 50 pseudorandom integers from 1 through 100,

(a) sampled without replacement

(b) sampled with replacement.

10 The following code simulates the sum (X) and difference (Y) of two uniform random variables $(U_1$ and $U_2)$. A scatterplot of Y versus X is then displayed and the correlation between X and Y is estimated.

```
> U2 <- runif(1000)
> U1 <- runif(1000)
> X <- U1 + U2
> Y <- U1 - U2
> plot(Y ~ X)
> cor(X,Y)          # this calculates the sample correlation
```

The correlation gives a measure of *linear* dependence between two random variables. A value near 0 indicates almost no such dependence, while a value near -1 or 1 indicates the existence of a linear relationship.

Execute the above code and use the output to answer the following questions.
(a) Do you think that X and Y are linearly dependent?
(b) Do you think that X and Y are stochastically independent? (To answer this, look carefully at the scatterplot.)
(c) Do you think that U_1 and U_2 are linearly dependent? (Perform an appropriate calculation to check.)
(d) Do you think that U_1 and U_2 are stochastically independent? (Obtain an appropriate plot to check.)

5.3 | Simulation of other random variables

5.3.1 Bernoulli random variables
A Bernoulli trial is an experiment in which there are only two possible outcomes. For example, a light bulb may work or not work; these are the only possibilities. Each outcome ("work" or "not work") has a probability associated with it; the sum of these two probabilities must be 1.

Example 5.4
Consider a student who guesses on a multiple choice test question which has five options; the student may guess correctly with probability 0.2 and incorrectly with probability 0.8. [The possible outcome of a guess is to either be correct or to be incorrect.]

Suppose we would like to know how well such a student would do on a multiple choice test consisting of 20 questions. We can get an idea by using simulation.

Each question corresponds to an independent Bernoulli trial with probability of success equal to 0.2. We can simulate the correctness of the student for each question by generating an independent uniform random number. If this number is less than 0.2, we say that the student guessed correctly; otherwise, we say that the student guessed incorrectly.

This will work, because the probability that a uniform random variable is less than 0.2 is exactly 0.2, while the probability that a uniform random variable exceeds 0.2 is exactly 0.8, which is the same as the probability that the student guesses incorrectly. Thus, the uniform random number generator is simulating the student. R can do this as follows:

```
> set.seed(23207) # use this to obtain our output
> guesses <- runif(20)
> correct.answers <- (guesses < 0.2)
> correct.answers
 [1] FALSE FALSE FALSE FALSE  TRUE  TRUE  TRUE FALSE  TRUE  TRUE FALSE
[12] FALSE FALSE FALSE FALSE FALSE FALSE FALSE  TRUE
```

The vector `correct.answers` is a logical vector which contains the results of the simulated student's guesses; a TRUE value corresponds to a correct guess, while a FALSE corresponds to an incorrect guess. The total number of correct guesses can be calculated.

```
> table(correct.answers)
correct.answers
FALSE   TRUE
   14      6
```

Our simulated student would score 6/20.

In the preceding example, we could associate the values "1" and "0" with the outcomes from a Bernoulli trial. This defines the Bernoulli random variable: a random variable which takes the value 1 with probability p, and 0 with probability $1 - p$.

The expected value of a Bernoulli random variable is p and its theoretical variance is $p(1 - p)$. In the above example, a student would expect to guess correctly 20% of the time; our simulated student was a little bit lucky, obtaining a mark of 30%.

Exercises

1 Write an R function which simulates the outcomes of a student guessing at a True–False test consisting of n questions.
   (a) Use the function to simulate one student guessing the answers to a test with 10 questions; calculate the number of correct answers for this student.
   (b) Simulate the number of correct answers for a student who guesses at a test with 1000 questions.

2 Suppose a class of 100 writes a 20-question True–False test, and everyone in the class guesses at the answers.
   (a) Use simulation to estimate the average mark on the test as well as the standard deviation of the marks.
   (b) Estimate the proportion of students who would obtain a mark of 30% or higher.

3 Write an R function which simulates 500 light bulbs, each of which has probability 0.99 of working. Using simulation, estimate the expected value and variance of the random variable X, which is 1 if the light bulb works and 0 if the light bulb does not work. What are the theoretical values?

4 Write an R function which simulates a binomial random variable with $n = 25$ and $p = 0.4$. (This is a sum of 25 independent Bernoulli (p) random variables.) By generating 100 of these binomial random variables, estimate the mean and variance of such a binomial random variable. (Compare with the theoretical values: 10, 6.)

5.3.2   Binomial random variables

Let X denote the sum of m independent Bernoulli random variables, each having probability p. X is called a binomial random variable; it represents the number of "successes" in m Bernoulli trials.

A binomial random variable can take values in the set $\{0, 1, 2, \ldots, m\}$. The probability of a binomial random variable X taking on any one of these values is governed by the binomial distribution:

$$P(X = x) = \binom{m}{x} p^x (1 - p)^{m-x}, \quad x = 0, 1, 2, \ldots, m.$$

These probabilities can be computed using the dbinom() function.

Syntax

```
dbinom(x, size, prob)
```

Here, size and prob are the binomial parameters m and p, respectively, while x denotes the number of "successes." The output from this function is the value of $P(X = x)$.

Example 5.5

Compute the probability of getting four heads in six tosses of a fair coin.

```
> dbinom(x = 4, size = 6, prob = 0.5)
[1] 0.234375
```

Thus, $P(X = 4) = 0.234$, when X is a binomial random variable with $m = 6$ and $p = 0.5$.

Cumulative probabilities of the form $P(X \leq x)$ can be computed using pbinom(); this function takes the same arguments as dbinom(). For example, we can calculate $P(X \leq 4)$ where X is the number of heads obtained in six tosses of a fair coin as:

```
> pbinom(4, 6, 0.5)
[1] 0.890625
```

The function qbinom() gives the quantiles for the binomial distribution. The 89th percentile of the distribution of X (as defined above) is:

```
> qbinom(0.89, 6, 0.5)
[1] 4
```

The expected value (or mean) of a binomial random variable is mp and the variance is $mp(1 - p)$.

The rbinom() function can be used to generate binomial pseudorandom numbers.

Syntax

```
rbinom(n, size, prob)
```

Here, size and prob are the binomial parameters, while n is the number of variates generated.

Example 5.6

Suppose 10% of the vacuum tubes produced by a machine are defective, and suppose 15 tubes are produced each hour. Each tube is independent of all other tubes. This process is judged to be out of control when more than four defective tubes are produced in any single hour. Simulate the number of defective tubes produced by the machine for each hour over a 24-hour period, and determine if any process should have been judged out of control at any point in that simulation run.

Since 15 tubes are produced each hour and each tube has a 0.1 probability of being defective, independent of the state of the other tubes, the number of defectives produced in one hour is a binomial random variable with $m = 15$ and $p = 0.1$. To simulate the number of defectives for each hour in a 24-hour period, we need to generate 24 binomial random numbers. We then identify all instances in which the number of defectives exceeds 5. One such simulation run is:

```
> defectives <- rbinom(24, 15, 0.1)
> defectives
 [1] 0 1 1 0 1 1 2 5 0 0 1 1 3 3 0 2 2 0 1 0 1 1 4 2
> any(defectives > 5)
[1] FALSE
```

Exercises

1 Suppose the proportion defective is 0.15 for a manufacturing operation. Simulate the number of defectives for each hour of a 24-hour period, assuming 25 units are produced each hour. Check if the number of defectives ever exceeds 5. Repeat, assuming $p = 0.2$ and then $p = 0.25$.

2 Simulate 10 000 binomial pseudorandom numbers with parameters 20 and 0.3, assigning them to a vector called `binsim`. Let X be a binomial $(20, 0.3)$ random variable. Use the simulated numbers to estimate the following:

(a) $P(X \le 5)$
(b) $P(X = 5)$
(c) $E[X]$
(d) $\text{Var}(X)$
(e) the 95th percentile of X (you may use the `quantile()` function)
(f) the 99th percentile of X
(g) the 99.9999th quantile of X.

In each case, compare your estimates with the true values. What is required to estimate extreme quantities accurately?

3 Use simulation to estimate the mean and variance of a binomial random variable with $n = 18$ and $p = 0.76$. Compare with the theoretical values.

4 Consider the following function which is designed to simulate binomial pseudorandom variates using the so-called *inversion* method:

```
> ranbin <- function(n, size, prob) {
+      cumpois <- pbinom(0:(size - 1), size, prob)
+      singlenumber <- function() {
```

```
+               x <- runif(1)
+               N <- sum(x > cumpois)
+               N
+           }
+           replicate(n, singlenumber())
+ }
```

(a) Study this function carefully and write documentation for it. Note, particularly, what the operations in the `singlenumber()` function are for.[4]

(b) Use `ranbin()` to simulate vectors of length 1000, 10 000, and 100 000 from the binomial distribution with size parameter 10 and probability parameter 0.4. Use the `system.time()` function to compare the execution times for these simulations with the corresponding execution times when `rbinom()` is used.

5 The following function simulates binomial pseudorandom numbers by summing up the corresponding independent Bernoulli random variables:

```
> ranbin2 <- function(n, size, prob) {
+       singlenumber <- function(size, prob) {
+           x <- runif(size)
+           N <- sum(x < prob)
+           N
+       }
+       replicate(n, singlenumber(size, prob))
+ }
```

(a) Study this function carefully and write documentation for it. Note, particularly, what the operations in the `singlenumber()` function are for.

(b) Use `ranbin2()` to simulate vectors of length 10 000 from the binomial distribution with size parameters 10, 100, and 1000, and probability parameter 0.4. Use the `system.time()` function to compare the execution times for these simulations with the corresponding execution times when `rbinom()` is used. Compare with execution times from the `ranbin()` function created in the previous exercise.

6 The generator in the previous exercise required `size` uniform pseudorandom numbers to be generated for each binomial number generated. The following generator is based on the same principle as the previous one, but only requires one uniform pseudorandom number to be generated for each binomial number generated:

```
> ranbin3 <- function(n, size, prob) {
+       singlenumber <- function(size, prob) {
+           k <- 0
+           U <- runif(1)
+           X <- numeric(size)
+           while (k < size) {
+               k <- k + 1
+               if (U <= prob) {
```

[4] The `replicate()` function allows us to repeatedly call `singlenumber()`, assigning n results to a vector. See `help(replicate)` for more information.

```
+                          X[k] <- 1
+                          U <- U / prob
+                  } else {
+                          X[k] <- 0
+                          U <- (U - prob)/(1 - prob)
+                  }
+              }
+              return(sum(X))
+          }
+          replicate(n, singlenumber(size, prob))
+ }
```

(a) Use the `ranbin3()` function to generate 100 pseudorandom numbers from binomial distributions with the following parameters:
   (i) `size` = 20 and `prob` = 0.4
   (ii) `size` = 500 and `prob` = 0.7.
(b) What is the conditional distribution of U/p, given that $U < p$?
(c) What is the conditional distribution of $(U - p)/(1 - p)$, given that $U > p$?
(d) Use the answers to the above questions to provide documentation for the `ranbin3()` function.

7 One version of the central limit theorem says that if X is a binomial random variable with parameters m and p, and

$$Z = \frac{X - mp}{\sqrt{mp(1 - p)}},$$

then Z is approximately standard normal, and the approximation improves as m gets large.
The following code simulates a large number of such Z values for values of m in the set $\{1, 2, \ldots, 100\}$ and plots a normal QQ-plot in each case:

```
> for (m in 1:100) {
+     z <- (rbinom(20000, size=m, prob=0.4) - m*0.4)/sqrt(m*0.4*0.6)
+     qqnorm(z, ylim=c(-4, 4), main=paste("QQ-plot, m= ", m))
+     qqline(z)
+ }
```

(a) Execute the code and observe how the distribution of Z changes as m increases.
(b) Modify the code so that a similar "movie" is produced for the cases where $p = 0.3, 0.2, 0.1, 0.05$, respectively. How large must m be before you see a reasonably straight line in the QQ-plot? Is $m = 100$ satisfactorily large in all cases?

5.3.3 Poisson random variables

The Poisson distribution is the limit of a sequence of binomial distributions with parameters n and p_n, where n is increasing to infinity, and p_n is decreasing to 0, but where the expected value (or mean) np_n converges to a constant λ. The variance $np_n(1 - p_n)$ converges to this same constant. Thus, the mean and variance of a Poisson random variable are both equal to λ. This parameter is sometimes referred to as a *rate*.

Poisson random variables arise in a number of different ways. They are often used as a crude model for count data. Examples of count data are the numbers of earthquakes in a region in a given year, or the number of individuals who arrive at a bank teller in a given hour. The limit comes from dividing the time period into n independent intervals, on which the count is either 0 or 1. The Poisson random variable is the total count.

The possible values that a Poisson random variable X could take are the nonnegative integers $\{0, 1, 2, \ldots\}$. The probability of taking on any of these values is

$$P(X = x) = \frac{e^{-x}\lambda^x}{x!}, \quad x = 0, 1, 2, \ldots.$$

These probabilities can be evaluated using the dpois() function.

Syntax

```
dpois(x, lambda)
```

Here, lambda is the Poisson rate parameter, while x is the number of Poisson events. The output from the function is the value of $P(X = x)$.

Example 5.7
According to the Poisson model, the probability of three arrivals at an automatic bank teller in the next minute, where the average number of arrivals per minute is 0.5, is

```
> dpois(x = 3, lambda = 0.5)
[1] 0.01263606
```

Therefore, $P(X = 3) = 0.0126$, if X is Poisson random variable with mean 0.5.

Cumulative probabilities of the form $P(X \leq x)$ can be calculated using ppois(), and Poisson quantiles can be computed using qpois().

We can generate Poisson random numbers using the rpois() function.

Syntax

```
rpois(n, lambda)
```

The parameter n is the number of variates produced, and lambda is as above.

Example 5.8
Suppose traffic accidents occur at an intersection with a mean rate of 3.7 per year. Simulate the annual number of accidents for a 10-year period, assuming a Poisson model.

```
> rpois(10, 3.7)
[1] 6 7 2 3 5 7 6 2 4 4
```

Poisson processes

A Poisson process is a simple model of the collection of events that occur during an interval of time. A way of thinking about a Poisson process is to think of a random collection of points on a line or in the plane (or in higher dimensions, if necessary).

The homogeneous Poisson process has the following properties:

1 The distribution of the number of points in a set is Poisson with rate proportional to the size of the set.
2 The numbers of points in non-overlapping sets are independent of each other.

In particular, for a Poisson process with rate λ the number of points on an interval $[0, T]$ is Poisson distributed with mean λT. One way to simulate this is as follows:

1 Generate N as a Poisson pseudorandom number with parameter λT.
2 Generate N independent uniform pseudorandom numbers on the interval $[0, T]$.

Example 5.9
Simulate points of a homogeneous Poisson process having a rate of 1.5 on the interval $[0, 10]$.

```
> N <- rpois(1, 1.5 * 10)
> P <- runif(N, max = 10)
> sort(P)
 [1] 0.03214420 0.11731867 0.25422972 2.43762063 3.93583254 4.05037783
 [7] 4.50931123 5.28833876 7.43922932 8.47007125 8.76151095 8.81578295
[13] 9.35800644
```

Exercises

1 Simulate the number of accidents for each year for 15 years, when the average rate is 2.8 accidents per year, assuming a Poisson model for numbers of accidents each year.
2 Simulate the number of surface defects in the finish of a sports car for 20 cars, where the mean rate is 1.2 defects per car.
3 Estimate the mean and variance of a Poisson random variable whose mean is 7.2 by simulating 10 000 Poisson pseudorandom numbers. Compare with the theoretical values.
4 Simulate vectors of 10 000 pseudorandom Poisson variates with mean 5, 10, 15, and 20, assigning the results to P5, P10, P15, and P20, respectively.
   (a) Estimate $E[\sqrt{X}]$ and $\text{Var}(\sqrt{X})$, where X is Poisson with rates $\lambda = 5, 10, 15$, and 20.
   (b) Noting that the variance of X increases with the mean of X, when X is a Poisson random variable, what is the effect of taking a square root of X on the relationship between the variance and the mean?

(Statisticians often take square roots of count data to 'stabilize the variance'; do you understand what this means?)

5 Conduct a simulation experiment to check the reasonableness of the assertion that the distribution of the number of points from a rate 1.5 Poisson process which fall in the interval $[4, 5]$ is Poisson with a mean of 1.5 by the following simulation. First, simulate a large number of realizations of the Poisson process on the interval $[0, 10]$. Then count the number of points in $[4, 5]$ for each realization. Compare this set of counts with simulated Poisson values using a QQ-plot. We supply the code for this below, and leave it to you to execute it and look at the resulting graph.

```
> poissonproc <- function() {
+       N <- rpois(1, 1.5 * 10)
+       P <- runif(N, max = 10)
+       return(sum( 4 <= P & P <= 5 ))
+ }
> counts <- replicate(10000, poissonproc())
> qqplot(counts, rpois(10000, 1.5))
> abline(0, 1) # the points lie reasonably close to this line
```

6 One version of the central limit theorem says that if X is a Poisson random variable with parameter λ, and

$$Z = \frac{X - \lambda}{\sqrt{\lambda}},$$

then Z is approximately standard normal, and the approximation improves as λ gets large.

The following code simulates a large number of such Z values for values of λ in the set $\{1, 3, \ldots, 99\}$ and plots a normal QQ-plot in each case:

```
> for (m in seq(1, 120, 2)) {
+       z <- (rpois(20000, lambda = m) - m) / sqrt(m)
+       qqnorm(z, ylim = c(-4, 4), main = "QQ-plot")
+       qqline(z)
+       mtext(bquote(lambda == .(m)), 3)    # this creates a subtitle which
+                                           # mixes mathematical and numerical notation
+ }
```

(a) Execute the code and observe how the distribution of Z changes as λ increases.

(b) How large must λ be before you see a reasonably straight line in the QQ-plot?

7 Simulate 10 000 realizations of a Poisson process with rate 2.5 on the interval $[0, 2]$.

(a) In each case, count the number of points in the subintervals $[0, 1]$ and $[1, 2]$.

(b) Are the counts in part (a) reasonably approximated by Poisson distributions with rate 2.5?

(c) Using an appropriate scatterplot, make a judgement as to whether it is reasonable to assume that the number of points in the interval $[0, 1]$ is independent of the number in $[1, 2]$. (In order for the scatterplot to be useful, it will be necessary to use the `jitter()` function.)

5.3.4 Exponential random numbers

Exponential random variables are used as simple models for such things as failure times of mechanical or electronic components, or for the time it takes a server to complete service to a customer. The exponential distribution is characterized by a constant *failure rate*, denoted by λ.

T has an exponential distribution with rate $\lambda > 0$ if

$$P(T \leq t) = 1 - e^{-\lambda t}$$

for any nonnegative t. The `pexp()` function can be used to evaluate this function.

Syntax
```
pexp(q, rate)
```

The output from this is the value of $P(T \leq q)$, where T is an exponential random variable with parameter `rate`.

Example 5.10
Suppose the service time at a bank teller can be modeled as an exponential random variable with a rate of 3 per minute. Then the probability of a customer being served in less than 1 minute is

```
> pexp(1, rate = 3)
[1] 0.950213
```

Thus, $P(X \leq 1) = 0.95$, when X is an exponential random variable with a rate of 3.

Differentiating the right-hand side of the distribution function with respect to t gives the exponential probability density function:

$$f(t) = \lambda e^{-\lambda t}.$$

The `dexp()` function can be used to evaluate this. It takes the same arguments as the `pexp()` function. The `qexp()` function can be used to obtain quantiles of the exponential distribution.

The expected value of an exponential random variable is $1/\lambda$, and the variance is $1/\lambda^2$.

A simple way to simulate exponential pseudorandom variates is based on the *inversion* method. For an exponential random variable $F(x) = 1 - e^{-\lambda x}$, so $F^{-1}(x) = -\frac{\log(1-U)}{\lambda}$. Therefore, for any $x \in (0, 1)$, we have

$$P(F(T) \leq x) = P(T \leq F^{-1}(x)) = F(F^{-1}(x)) = x.$$

Thus, $F(T)$ is a uniform random variable on the interval $(0, 1)$. Since we know how to generate uniform pseudorandom variates, we can obtain exponential variates by applying the inverse transformation $F^{-1}(x)$ to them.

That is, generate a uniform pseudorandom variable U on $[0,1]$, and set

$$1 - e^{-\lambda T} = U$$

Solving this for T, we have

$$T = -\frac{\log(1 - U)}{\lambda}.$$

T has an exponential distribution with rate λ.

The R function `rexp()` can be used to generate n random exponential variates.

Syntax
```
rexp(n, rate)
```

Example 5.11
A bank has a single teller who is facing a queue of 10 customers. The time for each customer to be served is exponentially distributed with rate 3 per minute. We can simulate the service times (in minutes) for the 10 customers.

```
> servicetimes <- rexp(10, rate = 3)
> servicetimes
 [1] 0.25415279 0.79177402 0.24280817 0.07887371 0.10738250 0.16583246
 [7] 0.83294959 0.09676131 0.16938459 0.53317718
```

The total time until these 10 simulated customers will complete service is around 3 minutes and 16 seconds:

```
> sum(servicetimes)
[1] 3.273096
```

Another way to simulate a Poisson process
It can be shown that the points of a homogeneous Poisson with rate λ process on the line are separated by independent exponentially distributed random variables with mean $1/\lambda$. This leads to another simple way of simulating a Poisson process on the line.

Example 5.12
Simulate the first 25 points of a Poisson 1.5 process, starting from 0.

```
> X <- rexp(25, rate = 1.5)
```

```
> cumsum(X)
 [1]  1.406436  1.608897  1.800167  3.044730  3.160853  3.640911
 [7]  4.827413  5.229759  6.542869  6.596817  7.305832  8.134470
```

```
[13]  10.704220 11.412163 11.515945 11.642972 12.277173 12.505261
[19]  15.205137 15.548352 16.727192 17.381278 17.678511 18.457350
[25]  18.658113
```

Exercises

1 Simulate 50 000 exponential random numbers having rate 3.
   (a) Find the proportion of these numbers which are less than 1. Compare with the probability that an exponential random variable with rate 3 will be less than 1.
   (b) Compute the average of these numbers. Compare with the expected value.
   (c) Calculate the variance of this sample, and compare with the theoretical value.

2 Suppose that a certain type of battery has a lifetime which is exponentially distributed with mean 55 hours. Use simulation to estimate the average and variance of the lifetime for this type of battery. Compare with the theoretical values.

3 A simple electronic device consists of two components which have failure times which may be modeled as independent exponential random variables. The first component has a mean time to failure of 3 months, and the second has a mean time to failure of 6 months. The electronic device will fail when either of the components fails. Use simulation to estimate the mean and variance of the time to failure for the device.

4 Re-do the calculation in the previous question under the assumption that the device will fail only when both components fail.

5 Simulate 10 000 realizations of a Poisson process with rate 2.5, using the method described in this section. Check that the distribution of the number of points in the interval $[0, 2]$ is reasonably close to a Poisson distribution with a mean of 5.

5.3.5 Normal random variables

A normal random variable X has a probability density function given by

$$f(x) = \frac{1}{\sigma\sqrt{2\pi}} e^{-\frac{(x-\mu)^2}{2\sigma^2}}$$

where μ is the expected value of X, and σ^2 denotes the variance of X. The *standard normal* random variable has mean $\mu = 0$ and standard deviation $\sigma = 1$.

The normal density function can be evaluated using the dnorm() function, the distribution function can be evaluated using pnorm(), and the quantiles of the normal distribution can be obtained using qnorm(). For example, the 95th percentile of the normal distribution with a mean of 2.7 and a standard deviation of 3.3 is:

```
> qnorm(0.95, mean = 2.7, sd = 3.3)
[1] 8.128017
```

Normal pseudorandom variables can be generated using the rnorm() function in R.

Syntax

```
rnorm(n, mean, sd)
```

This produces n normal pseudorandom variates which have mean mean and standard deviation sd.

Example 5.13
We can simulate 10 independent normal variates with a mean of -3 and a standard deviation of 0.5 using

```
> rnorm(10, -3, 0.5)
 [1] -3.520803 -3.130006 -2.682143 -2.330936 -3.158297 -3.293808
 [7] -3.171530 -2.815075 -2.783860 -2.899138
```

We can simulate random numbers from certain conditional distributions by first simulating according to an unconditional distribution, and then rejecting those numbers which do not satisfy the specified condition.

Example 5.14
Simulate x from the standard normal distribution, conditional on the event that $0 < x < 3$. We will simulate from the entire normal distribution and then accept only those values which lie between 0 and 3.
    We can simulate a large number of such variates as follows:

```
> x <- rnorm(100000)         # simulate from the standard normal
> x <- x[(0 < x) & (x < 3)]  # reject all x's outside (0,3)
> hist(x, probability=TRUE)  # show the simulated values
```

Figure 5.1 shows how the histogram tracks the rescaled normal density over the interval $(0, 3)$.

Exercises
1 Simulate 100 realizations of a normal random variable having a mean of 51 and a standard deviation of 5.2. Estimate the mean and standard deviation of your simulated sample and compare with the theoretical values.
2 Simulate 1000 realizations of a standard normal random variable Z, and use your simulated sample to estimate:
   (a) $P(Z > 2.5)$
   (b) $P(0 < Z < 1.645)$
   (c) $P(1.2 < Z < 1.45)$
   (d) $P(-1.2 < Z < 1.3)$.
   Compare with the theoretical values.

Histogram of x

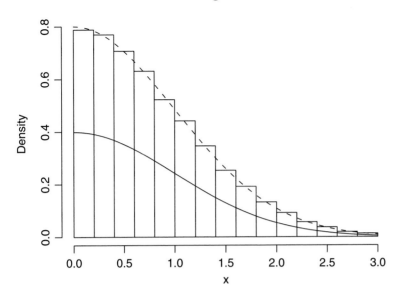

3 Simulate from the conditional distribution of a normal random variable X with a mean of 3 and a variance of 16, given that $|X| > 2$.

4 Using the fact that a χ^2 random variable on one degree of freedom has the same distribution as the square of a standard normal random variable, simulate 100 independent realizations of such a χ^2 random variable, and estimate its mean and variance. (Compare with the theoretical values: 1, 2.)

5 A χ^2 random variable on n degrees of freedom has the same distribution as the sum of n independent standard normal random variables. Simulate a χ^2 random variable with eight degrees of freedom, and estimate its mean and variance. (Compare with the theoretical values: 8, 16.)

5.4 | Monte Carlo integration

Suppose $g(x)$ is any function that is integrable on the interval $[a, b]$. The integral

$$\int_a^b g(x)\mathrm{d}x$$

gives the area of the region with $a < x < b$ and y between 0 and $g(x)$ (where negative values count towards negative areas).

Monte Carlo integration uses simulation to obtain approximations to these integrals. It relies on the law of large numbers. This law says that a sample mean from a large random sample will tend to be close to the expected value of the distribution being sampled. If we can express an integral as an expected value, we can approximate it by a sample mean.

For example, let $U_1, U_2, \ldots, U_n$ be independent uniform random variables on the interval $[a, b]$. These have density $f(u) = 1/(b - a)$ on that interval. Then

$$E[g(U_i)] = \int_a^b g(u) \frac{1}{b - a} du$$

so the original integral $\int_a^b g(x)dx$ can be approximated by $b - a$ times a sample mean of $g(U_i)$.

Example 5.15

To approximate the integral $\int_0^1 x^4 dx$, use the following lines:

```
> u <- runif(100000)
> mean(u^4)
[1] 0.2005908
```

Compare with the exact answer 0.2, which can easily be computed in this case.

Example 5.16

To approximate the integral $\int_2^5 sin(x)\, dx$, use the following lines:

```
> u <- runif(100000, min = 2, max = 5)
> mean(sin(u))*(5-2)
[1] -0.6851379
```

The true value can be shown to be -0.700.

Multiple integration

Now let $V_1, V_2, \ldots, V_n$ be an additional set of independent uniform random variables on the interval $[0, 1]$, and suppose $g(x, y)$ is now an integrable function of the two variables x and y. The law of large numbers says that

$$\lim_{n \to \infty} \sum_{i=1}^n g(U_i, V_i)/n = \int_0^1 \int_0^1 g(x, y)\, dx\, dy,$$

with probability 1.

So we can approximate the integral $\int_0^1 \int_0^1 g(x, y)\, dx\, dy$ by generating two sets of independent uniform pseudorandom variates, computing $g(U_i, V_i)$ for each one, and taking the average.

Example 5.17
Approximate the integral $\int_3^{10} \int_1^7 \sin(x - y) \, dx \, dy$ using the following:

```
> U <- runif(100000, min = 1, max = 7)
> V <- runif(100000, min = 3, max = 10)
> mean(sin(U - V))*42
[1] 0.07989664
```

The factor of $42 = (7 - 1)(10 - 3)$ compensates for the joint density of U and V being $f(u, v) = 1/42$.

The uniform density is by no means the only density that can be used in Monte Carlo integration. If the density of X is $f(x)$, then $E[g(X)/f(X)] = \int [g(x)/f(x)]f(x) \, dx = \int g(x) \, dx$ so we can approximate the latter by sample averages of $g(X)/f(X)$.

Example 5.18
To approximate the integral $\int_1^\infty \exp(-x^2) \, dx$, write it as the integral $\int_0^\infty \exp[-(x + 1)^2] \, dx$, and use an exponential distribution for X:

```
> X <- rexp(100000)
> mean( exp( -(X + 1)^2 ) / dexp(X) )
[1] 0.1401120
```

The true value of this integral is 0.1394.

Monte Carlo integration is not always successful: sometimes the ratio $g(X)/f(X)$ varies so much that the sample mean doesn't converge. Try to choose $f(x)$ so this ratio is roughly constant, and avoid situations where $g(x)/f(x)$ can be arbitrarily large.

Exercises

1 Use Monte Carlo integration to estimate the following integrals. Compare with the exact answer, if known.

$$\int_0^1 x \, dx \qquad \int_1^3 x^2 \, dx \qquad \int_0^\pi \sin(x) \, dx \qquad \int_1^\pi e^x \, dx \qquad \int_0^\infty e^{-x} \, dx$$

$$\int_0^\infty e^{-x^3} \, dx \qquad \int_0^3 \sin(e^x) \, dx \qquad \int_0^1 \frac{1}{\sqrt{2\pi}} e^{-x^2/2} \, dx$$

$$\int_0^2 \frac{1}{\sqrt{2\pi}} e^{-x^2/2} \, dx \qquad \int_0^3 \frac{1}{\sqrt{2\pi}} e^{-x^2/2} \, dx$$

2 Use Monte Carlo integration to estimate the following double integrals.

$$\int_0^1 \int_0^1 \cos(x - y) \, dx \, dy \qquad \int_0^1 \int_0^1 e^{-(y+x)^2}(x + y)^2 \, dx \, dy$$

$$\int_0^3 \int_0^1 \cos(x - y) \, dx \, dy \qquad \int_0^5 \int_0^2 e^{-(y+x)^2}(x + y)^2 \, dx \, dy$$

5.5 | Advanced simulation methods

The simulation methods discussed so far will only work for particular types of probability densities or distributions. General purpose simulation methods can be used to draw pseudorandom samples from a wide variety of distributions.

Example 5.19
Suppose X is a binomial (n, p) random variable with n known, but where the value of p is not known precisely; it is near 0.7. Given the data value $X = x$, we want to estimate p.

The maximum likelihood estimator for p is $\widehat{p} = x/n$, but this ignores our prior knowledge, i.e. the fact that p is really near 0.7.

If we convert our prior knowledge to a density, e.g. $p \sim N(0.7, \sigma = 0.1)$, Bayes' theorem lets us calculate the conditional density of p, given $X = x$, as:

$$f(p \mid X = x) \propto \exp\left(\frac{-(p - 0.7)^2}{2(0.1)^2}\right) p^x (1 - p)^{n-x}, \quad 0 < p < 1.$$

It is quite difficult to work out the constant that makes this a standard density integrating to 1, but numerical approximations (e.g. using Monte Carlo integration) are possible.

The goal of this section is to present simulation methods which can be used to generate pseudorandom numbers from a density like the one in the above example. Two simulation methods are commonly used:

- rejection sampling
- importance sampling.

5.5.1 Rejection sampling

The idea of rejection sampling was used in Section 5.3.5 to sample from a conditional distribution: sample from a convenient distribution, and select a subsample to achieve the target distribution. We will show how to use rejection sampling to draw a random sample from a univariate density or probability function $g(x)$, using a sequence of two examples.

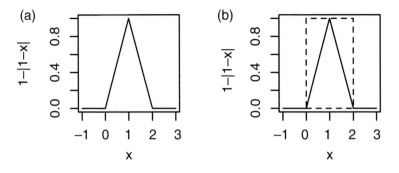

Our first example demonstrates the simplest version of rejection sampling.

Example 5.20

Simulate pseudorandom variates from the triangular density function

$$g(x) = \begin{cases} 1 - |1 - x|, & 0 \le x < 2 \\ 0, & \text{otherwise.} \end{cases}$$

The graph of the density function is displayed in Fig. 5.2(a). If we could draw points uniformly from the triangular region below the density, the x-coordinate would be distributed with density $g(x)$. Figure 5.2(b) shows that the graph where the density is nonzero can be entirely contained in a rectangle of height 1 and width 2. A subset of uniformly distributed points in the rectangle will be uniformly distributed in the triangular area under the triangular density. Thus, a strategy for simulating values from the triangular density is:

1 Simulate a point (U_1, U_2) uniformly in the rectangle.
2 If (U_1, U_2) is located within the triangular region, accept U_1 as a pseudorandom variate; otherwise, reject it, and return to step 1.

Since the triangular density occupies half of the area of the rectangle, we would expect to sample roughly two uniform points from the rectangle for every point we accept from the triangular distribution.

In vectorized form, the steps are:

```
> U1 <- runif(100000, max=2)
> U2 <- runif(100000)
> X <- U1[U2 < (1 - abs(1 - U1))]
```

The vector X will contain approximately 50 000 simulated values from the triangular distribution.

To accommodate situations where the density $g(x)$ might be nonzero on larger (possibly infinite) regions, and to increase the potential for computational efficiency, a more general form of rejection sampling is possible. Find a constant k, and density $f(x)$ from which we know how to sample, and for which $kg(x) \le f(x)$ for all x.

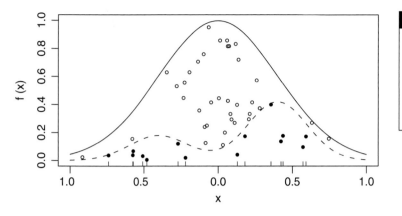

Fig. 5.3 Density $f(x)$ (solid line) and $kg(x)$ (dashed line). The points are uniformly distributed below $f(x)$; those above $kg(x)$ (open dots) are rejected, while those below (solid dots) are accepted. The tick marks show the output values of X.

Then we draw points uniformly below $kg(x)$ by taking a subsample of those drawn below $f(x)$ (see Figure 5.3):

```
repeat {
    draw X ~ f(X) , U ~ unif(0,1)
    if U * f(X) < kg(X)
        break
}
output X
```

Example 5.21

Simulate from the density $g(x) = Ce^{-x^{1.5}}$ for $x \geq 0$. The constant C is the unknown normalizing constant for this density. Even though we don't know C, since $0.5e^{-x^{1.5}} \leq e^{-x}$, we can use rejection sampling with $k = 0.5/C$:

```
> kg <- function(x) 0.5*exp(-(x^1.5))
> X <- rexp(100000)
> U <- runif(100000)
>                                  # accept only those X
> X <- X[ U*dexp(X) < kg(X) ]      # for which Uf(X) < kg(X)
```

The vector X now contains a large number of pseudorandom numbers from the required density. We can plot a histogram of these numbers as follows:

```
> hist(X, freq = FALSE, breaks="Scott")
```

We have chosen the relative frequency version of the histogram in order to overlay the theoretical density. The problem is that we don't know C to make $g(x)$ a density function. We could use Monte Carlo integration to find it, or more simply we can use the fact that we expect to accept a proportion k of the sampled points.

```
> k <- length(X) / 100000
> g <- function(x) kg(x) / k
> curve(g, from=0, to=max(X), add=TRUE)
```

Histogram of X

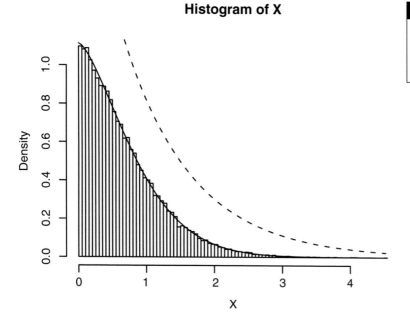

Fig. 5.4 Histogram of a sample from $g(x) = Ce^{-x^{1.5}}$. The approximate density $g(x)$ is shown with the solid line, and $f(x)/k$ is shown dashed.

```
> fbyk <- function(x) dexp(x) / k
> curve(fbyk, from=0, to=max(X), add=TRUE, lty=2)
```

The resulting graph is shown in Figure 5.4.

5.5.2 Importance sampling

A weighted average is an average in which observations are individually weighted. That is, instead of the usual sample average formula $\bar{x} = (1/n) \sum_{i=1}^{n} x_i$ we incorporate weights $w_1, \ldots, w_n$ and use $\bar{x}_w = \sum_{i=1}^{n} w_i x_i / \sum_{i=1}^{n} w_i$. The usual sample average can be seen to be a weighted average with all weights equal.

Importance sampling is a technique to generate both the sample and the weights randomly, in such a way that weighted averages approximate expected values with respect to a target density function $g(x)$. As with rejection sampling, we start by sampling from some other more convenient density $f(x)$:

1. Choose a convenient density $f(x)$ (which we know how to draw samples from).
2. Draw $(x_1, \ldots, x_n)$ as a sample from $f(x)$.
3. Calculate weights $w_i = g(x_i)/f(x_i)$.

We may now approximate the expectation of a function $h(X)$ where $X \sim g(x)$ using averages of $h(x_i)$ weighted by w_i.

One way to see why this works is to notice that w_i is proportional to the probability that a rejection sampler would accept x_i as a draw from $g(x)$. Given x_i, the contribution $w_i h(x_i) / \sum_{i=1}^{n} w_i$ in the weighted average formula is exactly the expected contribution from this draw to a sample mean if we were using rejection sampling. We know rejection sampling works, so importance sampling must work too. It may even be more efficient, in that we don't throw away information from rejected draws. In addition, it is not necessary to find the constant k as in rejection sampling. Neither $g(x_i)$ nor $f(x_i)$ need be normalized densities: dividing by the sum of the weights automatically provides the appropriate scaling.

On the other hand, working with weighted samples is more difficult than working with simple random samples, so in many cases rejection sampling would be preferred.

We illustrate these issues by continuing with the example from the previous section. We may approximate the mean and variance of the density $g(x)$ from that section using the `weighted.mean` function:

```
> X <- rexp(100000)
> W <- g(X)/dexp(X)
> mean <- weighted.mean(X, W)
> mean
[1] 0.6579574
> weighted.mean( (X - mean)^2, W )   # The variance as E[ (X - Xbar)^2 ]
[1] 0.3036045
```

Exercises

1 Write a function to generate standard normal pseudorandom numbers on the interval $[-4,4]$, using `runif()` and the rejection method. Can you modify the function so that it can generate standard normal pseudorandom numbers on the entire real line?

2 The following function returns normal pseudorandom numbers:

```
> rannorm <- function(n, mean = 0, sd = 1){
+       singlenumber <- function() {
+           repeat{
+           U <- runif(1)
+           U2 <- sign(runif(1, min = -1))      # value is +1 or -1
+           Y <- rexp(1) * U2          # Y is a double exponential r.v.
+           if (U < dnorm(Y) / exp(-abs(Y))) break
+           }
+           return(Y)
+       }
+       replicate(n, singlenumber()) * sd + mean
+ }
```

(a) Use this function to generate a vector of 10 000 normal pseudo-random numbers with a mean of 8 and standard deviation 2.

(b) Obtain a QQ-plot to check the accuracy of this generator.

(c) Use the `curve()` function to draw the graph of the standard normal density on the interval $[0, 4]$. Use the add = TRUE parameter to overlay the exponential density on the same interval to verify that the rejection method has been implemented appropriately.

3 Consider the following two methods for simulating from the discrete distribution with values 0, 1, 2, 3, 4, 5 which take respective probabilities 0.2, 0.3, 0.1, 0.15, 0.05, 0.2.
The first method is an inversion method:

```
> probs <- c(0.2, 0.3, 0.1, 0.15, 0.05, 0.2)
> randiscrete1 <- function(n, probs) {
+       cumprobs <- cumsum(probs)
+       singlenumber <- function() {
+           x <- runif(1)
+           N <- sum(x > cumprobs)
+           N
+       }
+       replicate(n, singlenumber())
+ }
```

The second method is a rejection method:

```
> randiscrete2 <- function(n, probs) {
+       singlenumber <- function() {
+           repeat{
+               U <- runif(2, min=c(-0.5, 0), max=c(length(probs) - 0.5,
+                          max(probs)))
+               if (U[2] < probs[round(U[1]) + 1]) break
+           }
+           return(round(U[1]))
+       }
+       replicate(n, singlenumber())
+ }
```

Execute both functions using $n = 100, 1000$, and 10 000. Use `system.time()` to determine which method is faster.

4 Repeat the above exercise using the probability distribution on the integers $\{0, 1, 2, \ldots, 99\}$ defined by

```
> set.seed(91626)
> probs <- runif(100)
> probs <- probs / sum(probs)
```

When is rejection sampling preferred to the inversion method for discrete distributions?

5 Write a function which generates a weighted sample of binomial (m, p) pseudorandom numbers using importance sampling. Compare the weighted average to the theoretical mean.

Chapter exercises

1 Write a function which simulates two people (Ann and Bob) playing table tennis. (Assume that the first person to reach 21 points wins the game.)

(a) Begin with the assumption that each player successively hits the ball with probability p_{Ann} and p_{Bob}, respectively. Find the probability that Ann will win for various values of these probabilities.

(b) Add more features, such as an ability to serve, or to smash, or spin the ball. Use your imagination.

2 The following model has been used for the study of contagion.[5] Suppose that there are N persons some of whom are sick with influenza. The following assumptions are made:

• when a sick person meets a healthy one, the chance is α that the latter will be infected
• all encounters are between two persons
• all possible encounters in pairs are equally likely
• one such encounter occurs in every unit of time.

(a) Write a function which simulates this model for various values of N (say, 10 000) and α (say, between 0.001 and 0.1). Monitor the history of this process, assuming that one individual is infected at the beginning.

(b) Suppose that initially only one individual is infected. What is the expected length of time until 1000 people are infected?

(c) Now add the assumption that each infected person has a 0.01 chance of recovering at each time unit. Monitor several histories of this new process, and compare them with the histories of the old process.

(d) Re-do with the assumption that the time between encounters is an exponential random variable with a mean of 5 minutes.

(e) Re-do assuming that the time between encounters is the absolute value of a normal random variable with a mean of 5 minutes and a standard deviation of 1 minute.

3 Simulate the following simple model of auto insurance claims:

• Claims arise according to a Poisson process at a rate of 100 per year.
• Each claim is a random size following a gamma distribution with shape and rate parameters both equal to 2. This distribution has a mean of 1 and a variance of 1/2. Claims must be paid by the insurance company as soon as they arise.
• The insurance company earns premiums at a rate of 105 per year, spread evenly over the year (i.e. at time t measured in years, the total premium received is 105t.)

Write R code to do the following:

(a) Simulate the times and amounts of all the claims that would occur in one year. Draw a graph of the total amount of money that the insurance company would have through the year, starting from zero: it should increase smoothly with the premiums, and drop at each claim time.

(b) Repeat the simulation 1000 times, and estimate the following quantities:

(i) The expected minimum amount of money that the insurance company would have.

(ii) The expected final amount of money that the insurance company would have.

4 Let $f(x) = (\sin x)^2$ for $0 < x < 2\pi$.

(a) Graph the function.

(b) Use Monte Carlo integration to find the area under $f(x)$ on the range $0 < x < 2\pi$, and to find a 95% confidence interval for the area.

(c) Use trigonometry or calculus to find the same area exactly. Did the confidence interval cover the true value?

(d) Write a function called `rsin2` which generates random values from the density $f(x)/k$, $0 < x < 2\pi$, where k is the area found above. The function should take a single argument specifying how many samples are required, e.g. `rsin2(10)` would return a vector of 10 samples from this distribution. Use the rejection method to draw the samples. Plot a histogram based on 1000 samples.

(e) Use your function to draw a sample of 1 000 000 samples, and calculate a 95% confidence interval for the mean. (By symmetry, the true mean must be π. Did your confidence interval cover the true value?)

## 6

Computational linear algebra

Linear algebra deals with vector spaces and linear operations on them. In mathematics, we usually represent vectors as column vectors of numbers, and linear operations as matrices. Applying a linear operation to a vector becomes multiplication of a column vector by a matrix, and composition of operations is matrix multiplication.

One of the most important applications of linear algebra is in solving systems of linear equations. For example, we represent the system

$$
\begin{aligned}
3x_1 - 4x_2 &= 6 \\
x_1 + 2x_2 &= -3
\end{aligned}
$$

as

$$Ax = b,$$

where

$$
A = \begin{bmatrix} 3 & -4 \\ 1 & 2 \end{bmatrix}, \quad x = \begin{bmatrix} x_1 \\ x_2 \end{bmatrix}, \quad b = \begin{bmatrix} 6 \\ -3 \end{bmatrix},
$$

and solve it as

$$
x = A^{-1}b = \begin{bmatrix} 0.2 & 0.4 \\ -0.1 & 0.3 \end{bmatrix} \begin{bmatrix} 6 \\ -3 \end{bmatrix} = \begin{bmatrix} 0 \\ -1.5 \end{bmatrix}.
$$

Linear algebra is also extensively used in statistics in linear regression, smoothing, simulation, and so on. We will touch on some of these applications in this book, but most of them are beyond our scope.

From a computational point of view, many of the issues in linear algebra come down to solving systems of linear equations efficiently and accurately. In order to assess accuracy we need to understand properties of the matrices; this understanding is valuable in itself. Efficiency often means formulating problems differently than we would from a strict mathematical point of view. For example, as we will see below, we would not normally solve $Ax = b$ using the mathematical solution $x = A^{-1}b$: computationally, this is both inefficient and inaccurate.

In this chapter, we will present several approaches to this problem, and illustrate them with R code. R incorporates routines for linear algebra computations from the *LINPACK*[1] and *LAPACK*[2] libraries. These are well-tested, well-trusted libraries, so R is an excellent platform for computational linear algebra. However, as with all numerical computation, understanding the underlying theory is essential in order to obtain reliable results.

6.1 Vectors and matrices in R

Numeric "vector" and "matrix" objects in R are a close match to mathematical vectors and matrices. (R also allows other types of data in its vectors and matrices, but that won't concern us here.) R normally makes no distinction between column vectors and row vectors, though it does allow matrices with one column or one row when this distinction is important.

Numeric matrices in R are printed as rectangular arrays of numbers, but are stored internally as vectors with dimension attributes. For the purpose of computational linear algebra, the internal storage can usually be ignored.

6.1.1 Constructing matrix objects

Matrices can be constructed using the functions `matrix()`, `cbind()` or `rbind()`.

Syntax
```
matrix(data, nrow, ncol)   # data is a vector of nrow*ncol values
cbind(d1, d2, ..., dm)     # d1, ..., dm are vectors (columns)
rbind(d1, d2, ..., dn)     # d1, ..., dn are vectors (rows)
```

Example 6.1
Hilbert matrices are often studied in numerical linear algebra because they are easy to construct but have surprising properties.

```
> H3 <- matrix(c(1, 1/2, 1/3, 1/2, 1/3, 1/4, 1/3, 1/4, 1/5), nrow=3)
> H3
          [,1]      [,2]      [,3]
[1,] 1.0000000 0.5000000 0.3333333
[2,] 0.5000000 0.3333333 0.2500000
[3,] 0.3333333 0.2500000 0.2000000
```

Here H3 is the 3×3 Hilbert matrix, where entry (i,j) is $1/(i+j-1)$. Note that `ncol` is not required in the command that created it, since the `data` argument has been assigned a vector consisting of nine elements; it is clear that if there are three rows there must also be three columns.

We could also construct this matrix by binding columns together as follows:

```
> 1/cbind(seq(1, 3), seq(2, 4), seq(3, 5))
          [,1]      [,2]      [,3]
[1,] 1.0000000 0.5000000 0.3333333
[2,] 0.5000000 0.3333333 0.2500000
[3,] 0.3333333 0.2500000 0.2000000
```

[1] Dongarra, J. J., Bunch, J. R., Moler, C. B. and Stewart, G. W. (1978) *LINPACK Users Guide*. Philadelphia: SIAM.

[2] Anderson, E. *et al.* (1999) *LAPACK Users' Guide*, 3rd edition. Philadelphia: SIAM. Available on-line at www.netlib.org/lapack/lug/lapack_lug.html.

In this example, `rbind()` would give the same result, because of symmetry.

___

Matrices are not necessarily square.

___

Example 6.2
For some simple non-square examples, consider

```
> matrix(seq(1, 12), nrow=3)
     [,1] [,2] [,3] [,4]
[1,]    1    4    7   10
[2,]    2    5    8   11
[3,]    3    6    9   12
```

and

```
> x <- seq(1, 3)
> x2 <- x^2
> X <- cbind(x, x2)
> X
     x x2
[1,] 1  1
[2,] 2  4
[3,] 3  9
```

The matrix X, above, could also have been constructed as

```
> X <- matrix(c(1, 2, 3, 1, 4, 9), ncol=2)
```

though it will print differently, because we haven't entered any column names.

___

Exercises
1 Use the `matrix()`, `seq()` and `rep()` functions to construct the following 5×5 *Hankel* matrix:

$$A = \begin{bmatrix} 1 & 2 & 3 & 4 & 5 \\ 2 & 3 & 4 & 5 & 6 \\ 3 & 4 & 5 & 6 & 7 \\ 4 & 5 & 6 & 7 & 8 \\ 5 & 6 & 7 & 8 & 9 \end{bmatrix}.$$

Convert the code into a function which can be used to construct matrices of dimension $n \times n$ which have the same pattern. Use the function to output 10×10 and 12×12 Hankel matrices.

2 Use `rbind()` to stack the vectors [0.1 0.5 0.0 0.4], [0.2 0.3 0.5 0.0], [0.3 0.0 0.5 0.2], and [0.2 0.3 0.2 0.3] into a 4 × 4 matrix. Assign the result to an object called P.

3 Use `cbind()` to construct the 7 × 3 matrix:

$$
W = \begin{bmatrix}
1 & 2 & 4 \\
1 & 3 & 7 \\
1 & 4 & 5 \\
1 & 5 & 6 \\
1 & 6 & 7 \\
1 & 7 & 5 \\
1 & 8 & 3
\end{bmatrix}.
$$

6.1.2   Accessing matrix elements; row and column names

Indexing of matrix elements is the same as for data frames: the (i, j) element is located in the ith row and jth column. For example, the $(3, 2)$ element of X is 9. We can access this element using

```
> X[3, 2]
[1] 9
```

We can access the ith row using `X[i, ]`, and the jth column using `X[, j]`. For example,

```
> X[3,]
 x  x2
 3   9
> X[, 2]
[1] 1 4 9
```

When we do this, the result is usually a vector, with no dimension information kept. If we want to maintain the result as a row or column vector, we use the optional `drop = FALSE` argument when we index:

```
> X[3, , drop = FALSE]
      x  x2
[1,]  3   9
> X[, 2, drop = FALSE]
      x2
[1,]   1
[2,]   4
[3,]   9
```

As X shows, it is possible for the rows and/or columns of a matrix to have individual names. For example,

```
> colnames(X)
[1] "x"   "x2"
```

In this example, the rows do not have names:

```
> rownames(X)
NULL
```

We can assign names using

```
> rownames(X) <- c("obs1", "obs2", "obs3")
> X
     x x2
obs1 1  1
obs2 2  4
obs3 3  9
```

Internally, R stores matrices and data frames quite differently. Matrices are stored as a single vector of values with an associated dimension attribute, while data frames are stored as lists of columns. Because of this, the `$` extraction function does not work for matrices. For example,

```
> X$x
NULL
```

However, it is possible to use the row or column names to access rows or columns as in the following example:

```
> X[, "x"]
obs1 obs2 obs3
   1    2    3
```

Exercises

1 Construct the *stochastic matrix*[3] that appears below.

```
      sunny rainy
sunny  0.2   0.8
rainy  0.3   0.7
```

2 Construct the two vectors of heights (in cm) and weights (in kg) for 5 individuals:

```
> height <- c(172, 168, 167, 175, 180)
> weight <- c(62, 64, 51, 71, 69)
```

Bind these vectors into a matrix, and modify the result to obtain:

```
        height weight
Neil      172    62
Cindy     168    64
Pardeep   167    51
Deepak    175    71
Hao       180    69
```

3 Refer to the previous exercise. Pardeep's height is really 162 cm, Hao's height is really 181 cm and his weight is really 68 kg. Correct the matrix accordingly.

[3] A stochastic matrix has the properties that all entries are nonnegative and the rows sum to 1. Such a matrix is used to describe transition probabilities for a *Markov chain*. In this example, we might be thinking of the weather on a sequence of days; if it is sunny today, the probability of a sunny day tomorrow is 0.2, and if it is rainy today, the probability of a sunny day tomorrow is 0.3.

6.1.3 Matrix properties

The dimension of a matrix is its number of rows and its number of columns. For example,

```
> dim(X)
[1] 3 2
```

Recall that the determinant of a 2×2 matrix $\begin{bmatrix} a & b \\ c & d \end{bmatrix}$ can be calculated as $ad - bc$. For larger square matrices, the calculation becomes more complicated. It can be found in R using the det() function, as in

```
> det(H3)
[1] 0.000462963
```

The diagonal elements can be obtained using the diag() function, as in

```
> diag(X)
[1] 1 4
> diag(H3)
[1] 1.0000000 0.3333333 0.2000000
```

We can then compute the trace (the sum of the diagonal entries) using a home-made function such as

```
> trace <- function(data) sum(diag(data))
```

Applying this function to the matrices constructed in Examples 6.1 and 6.2, we obtain

```
> trace(X)
[1] 5
> trace(H3)
[1] 1.533333
```

The diag() function can also be used to turn a vector into a square diagonal matrix whose diagonal elements correspond to the entries of the given vector. For example,

```
> diag(diag(H3))
     [,1]       [,2] [,3]
[1,]    1 0.0000000  0.0
[2,]    0 0.3333333  0.0
[3,]    0 0.0000000  0.2
```

The t() function is used to calculate the matrix transpose X^T:

```
> t(X)
   obs1 obs2 obs3
x     1    2    3
x2    1    4    9
```

Exercises

1 Verify that $\det(A) = \det(A^T)$ by experimenting with several matrices A.

2 A matrix A is said to be *skew-symmetric* if

$$A^T = -A.$$

Construct a 3×3 skew-symmetric matrix and verify that its determinant is 0. What is the trace of your matrix?

6.1.4 Triangular matrices

The functions `lower.tri()` and `upper.tri()` can be used to obtain the lower and upper triangular parts of matrices. The output of the functions is a matrix of logical elements, with TRUE representing the relevant triangular elements. For example,

```
> lower.tri(H3)
       [,1]   [,2]   [,3]
[1,]  FALSE  FALSE  FALSE
[2,]   TRUE  FALSE  FALSE
[3,]   TRUE   TRUE  FALSE
```

We can obtain the lower triangular matrix whose nonzero elements match the lower triangular elements of H3 by using

```
> Hnew <- H3
> Hnew[upper.tri(H3, diag=TRUE)] <- 0 # diag=TRUE causes all
>                                     # diagonal elements to be
>                                     # included
> Hnew
             [,1]   [,2] [,3]
[1,]  0.0000000 0.00     0
[2,]  0.5000000 0.00     0
[3,]  0.3333333 0.25     0
```

Exercises

1 Obtain a matrix which has the same upper triangular part as H3 (including the diagonal) but is 0 below the diagonal.

2 Check the output from

```
> Hnew[lower.tri(H3)]
```

Is it what you expected?

3 With X as defined in Section 6.2, what difference would you expect between X[3, 2] and X[3, 2, drop=FALSE]? Use R to calculate the dimension of each of these expressions.

6.1.5 Matrix arithmetic

Multiplication of a matrix by a scalar constant is the same as multiplication of a vector by a constant. For example, using the X matrix from the previous section, we can multiply each element by 2 as in

```
> Y <- 2 * X
> Y
```

```
      x x2
obs1 2   2
obs2 4   8
obs3 6  18
```

Elementwise addition of matrices also proceeds as for vectors. For example,

```
> Y + X
      x x2
obs1 3   3
obs2 6  12
obs3 9  27
```

When adding matrices, always ensure that the dimensions match properly. If they do not match correctly, an error message will appear, as in

```
> t(Y) + X
Error in t(Y) + X : non-conformable arrays
```

In this example, Y^T is a 2×3 matrix while X is 3×2.

The command X * Y performs elementwise multiplication. Note that this differs from the usual form of matrix multiplication that we will discuss below. For example,

```
> X * Y
       x   x2
obs1   2    2
obs2   8   32
obs3  18  162
```

Again, in order for this kind of multiplication to work, the dimensions of the matrices must match.

6.2 | Matrix multiplication and inversion

If A and B are matrices, then the matrix product AB is the matrix representing the composition of the two operations: first apply B, then apply A to the result. For matrix multiplication to be a properly defined operation, the matrices to be multiplied must *conform*. That is, the number of columns of the first matrix must match the number of rows of the second matrix. The resulting matrix AB will have its row dimension taken from A and its column dimension taken from B.

In R, this form of matrix multiplication can be performed using the operator %*%, for example

```
> t(Y) %*% X
      x   x2
x    28   72
x2   72  196
```

From the previous section we saw that t(Y) has three columns and X has three rows, so we can perform the multiplication $Y^T X$. The result is a 2×2 matrix, since t(Y) has two rows and X has two columns.

If we failed to transpose Y, we would obtain an error, as in

```
> Y %*% X
Error in Y %*% X : non-conformable arguments
```

The crossprod() function is a somewhat more efficient way to calculate $Y^T X$:

```
> crossprod(Y, X)
    x    x2
x   28   72
x2  72  196
```

Note that the first argument of crossprod() is transposed automatically. The reason this is more efficient than t(Y) %*% X is that the latter needs to make a new object t(Y) before performing the multiplication. If Y is a large matrix, this will consume a lot of memory and noticeable computation time. The crossprod(Y, X) function call can access the elements of Y directly, since the (i,j) element of Y^T is simply the (j,i) element of Y.

Exercises

1 Compute $1.5X$, using the matrix X discussed in Section 6.2.

2 Use the crossprod() function to compute $X^T X$ and XX^T. Note the dimensions of the resulting products.

6.2.1 Matrix inversion

The inverse of a square $n \times n$ matrix A, denoted by A^{-1}, is the solution to the matrix equation $AA^{-1} = I$, where I is the $n \times n$ identity matrix. We can view this as n separate systems of linear equations in n unknowns, whose solutions are the columns of A^{-1}. For example, with

$$A = \begin{bmatrix} 3 & -4 \\ 1 & 2 \end{bmatrix},$$

the matrix equation

$$\begin{bmatrix} 3 & -4 \\ 1 & 2 \end{bmatrix} \begin{bmatrix} b_{11} & b_{12} \\ b_{21} & b_{22} \end{bmatrix} = \begin{bmatrix} 1 & 0 \\ 0 & 1 \end{bmatrix}$$

is equivalent to the two equations:

$$\begin{bmatrix} 3 & -4 \\ 1 & 2 \end{bmatrix} \begin{bmatrix} b_{11} \\ b_{21} \end{bmatrix} = \begin{bmatrix} 1 \\ 0 \end{bmatrix},$$

and

$$\begin{bmatrix} 3 & -4 \\ 1 & 2 \end{bmatrix} \begin{bmatrix} b_{12} \\ b_{22} \end{bmatrix} = \begin{bmatrix} 0 \\ 1 \end{bmatrix}.$$

The usual computational approach to finding A^{-1} involves solving these two equations.

However, this is not always a good idea! Often the reason we are trying to find A^{-1} is so that we can solve a system $Ax = b$ with the solution $x = A^{-1}b$. It doesn't make sense from a computational point of view to solve n systems of linear equations in order to obtain a result which will be used as the solution to one system. If we know how to solve systems, we should use that knowledge to solve $Ax = b$ directly. Furthermore, using A^{-1} may give a worse approximation to the final result than the direct approach, because there are so many more operations involved, giving opportunties for much more rounding error to creep into our results.

6.2.2 The *LU* decomposition

The general strategy for solving a system of equations $Ax = b$ is to break down the problem into simpler ones. This often involves rewriting the matrix A in a special form; one such form is called the *LU* decomposition.

In the *LU* decomposition, we write A as a product of two matrices L and U. The matrix L is lower triangular with unit values on the diagonal, i.e.

$$
L = \begin{bmatrix}
1 & 0 & \cdots & 0 \\
l_{21} & 1 & \ddots & \vdots \\
\vdots & & \ddots & 0 \\
l_{n1} & l_{n2} & \cdots & 1
\end{bmatrix}.
$$

U is upper triangular, i.e.

$$
U = \begin{bmatrix}
u_{11} & u_{12} & \cdots & u_{1n} \\
0 & u_{22} & \cdots & u_{2n} \\
\vdots & \ddots & \ddots & \vdots \\
0 & \cdots & 0 & u_{nn}
\end{bmatrix}.
$$

It turns out that this factorization of A is quite easy to find by stepping through the entries one by one. For example, if

$$
A = \begin{bmatrix}
2 & 4 & 3 \\
6 & 16 & 10 \\
4 & 12 & 9
\end{bmatrix},
$$

the calculations would proceed as follows, where we write the entries of A as a_{ij}. We make repeated use of the relation

$$
a_{ij} = \sum_{k=1}^{3} l_{ik} u_{kj},
$$

and take advantage of knowing the 0's and 1's in L and U:

1 $a_{11} = 2 = l_{11} \times u_{11} = 1 \times u_{11}$, so $u_{11} = 2$
2 $a_{21} = 6 = l_{21} \times u_{11} = l_{21} \times 2$, so $l_{21} = 3$

3 $a_{31} = 4 = l_{31} \times u_{11} = l_{31} \times 2$, so $l_{31} = 2$

4 $a_{12} = 4 = l_{11} \times u_{12}$, so $u_{12} = 4$

5 $a_{22} = 16 = l_{21} \times u_{12} + l_{22} \times u_{22} = 3 \times 4 + 1 \times u_{22}$, so $u_{22} = 4$

6 $a_{32} = 12 = l_{31} \times u_{12} + l_{32} \times u_{22} = 2 \times 4 + l_{32} \times 4$, so $l_{32} = 1$

7 $a_{13} = 3 = l_{11} \times u_{13} = 1 \times u_{13}$, so $u_{13} = 3$

8 $a_{23} = 10 = l_{21} \times u_{13} + l_{22} \times u_{23} = 3 \times 3 + 1 \times u_{23}$, so $u_{23} = 1$

9 $a_{33} = 9 = l_{31} \times u_{13} + l_{32} \times u_{23} + l_{33} \times u_{33} = 2 \times 3 + 1 \times 1 + 1 \times u_{33}$,
so $u_{33} = 2$.

Once we have L and U in hand, solving the system of equations $Ax = b$ is easy. We write the system as $L(Ux) = b$, set $y = Ux$ and solve $Ly = b$ for y first. Because L is lower triangular, this is straightforward using a procedure known as *forward elimination*. Continuing the example above, with $b = [-1, -2, -7]^T$, and setting $y = [y_1, y_2, y_3]^T$, we make use of the relation

$$b_i = \sum_{j=1}^{3} l_{ij} y_j$$

to calculate:

10 $b_1 = -1 = l_{11} \times y_1 = 1 \times y_1$, so $y_1 = -1$

11 $b_2 = -2 = l_{21} \times y_1 + l_{22} \times y_2 = 3 \times (-1) + 1 \times y_2$, so $y_2 = 1$

12 $b_3 = -7 = l_{31} \times y_1 + l_{32} \times y_2 + l_{33} \times y_3 = 2 \times (-1) + 1 \times 1 + 1 \times y_3$,
so $y_3 = -6$.

Finally, we solve $Ux = y$. This time the fact that U is upper triangular means solving for the entries in reverse order is easy, using a procedure called *back substitution*:

13 $y_3 = -6 = u_{33} \times x_3 = 2 \times x_3$, so $x_3 = -3$

14 $y_2 = 1 = u_{22} \times x_2 + u_{23} \times x_3 = 4 \times x_2 + 1 \times (-3)$, so $x_2 = 1$

15 $y_1 = -1 = u_{11} \times x_1 + u_{12} \times x_2 + u_{13} \times x_3 = 2 \times x_1 + 4 \times 1 + 3 \times (-3)$,
so $x_1 = 2$.

By processing these steps successively, the problem of solving $Ax = b$ has been reduced to solving 15 successive linear equations, each with just one unknown. The procedure is easily automated. In fact, the default method used in R for solving linear equations is based on this technique; the only substantial difference is that the ordering of the columns is rearranged before factoring so that rounding error is minimized.

6.2.3 Matrix inversion in R

In R, matrices are inverted and linear systems of equations are solved using the `solve()` or `qr.solve()` functions. `solve()` uses a method based on the *LU* decomposition; `qr.solve()` is based on the *QR* decomposition that is described below.

As an example, we compute the inverse of the 3×3 Hilbert matrix introduced in Section 6.1:

```
> H3inv <- solve(H3)
```

```
> H3inv
      [,1]  [,2]  [,3]
[1,]     9  -36    30
[2,]   -36  192  -180
[3,]    30 -180   180
```

To verify that this is the inverse of H3, we can check that the product of H3inv and H3 is the 3×3 identity:

```
> H3inv %*% H3
           [,1]          [,2]          [,3]
[1,]  1.000000e+00  8.881784e-16   6.882515e-16
[2,] -3.774758e-15  1.000000e+00  -3.420875e-15
[3,]  6.144391e-15  0.000000e+00   1.000000e+00
```

The diagonal elements are all 1's, but five of the off-diagonal elements are nonzero. Scientific notation is used for these elements; they are all computed to be of the order of 10^{-14} or smaller. They are "numerically" close to 0. H3inv is not the exact inverse of H3, but it is believable that it is very close.

Exercises
1 Compute the inverse of $X^T X$. Verify your result using crossprod().
2 Can you compute the inverse of XX^T? Why is there a problem?
3 The general $n \times n$ Hilbert matrix has (i, j) element given by $1/(i+j-1)$.
   (a) Write a function which gives the $n \times n$ Hilbert matrix as its output, for any positive integer n.
   (b) Are all of the Hilbert matrices invertible?
   (c) Use solve() and qr.solve() to compute the inverse of the Hilbert matrices, up to $n = 10$. Is there a problem?

6.2.4 Solving linear systems
The function solve(A, b) gives the solution to systems of equations of the form $Ax = b$. For example, let us find x such that $H_3 x = b$ where H_3 is the 3×3 Hilbert matrix and $b = [1 \ 2 \ 3]^T$.

```
> b <- c(1, 2, 3)
> x <- solve(H3, b)
> x
[1]    27 -192   210
```

In other words, the solution vector is $x = [27, -192, 210]^T$.

Exercise
1 Let $[x_1, x_2, x_3, x_4, x_5, x_6]^T = [10, 11, 12, 13, 14, 15]^T$. Find the coefficients of the quintic polynomial $f(x)$ for which $[f(x_1), f(x_2), f(x_3), f(x_4), f(x_5), f(x_6)]^T = [25, 16, 26, 19, 21, 20]^T$. (Hint: the quintic polynomial $f(x) = a_0 + a_1 x + a_2 x^2 + a_3 x^3 + a_4 x^4 + a_5 x^5$ can be viewed as the matrix product of the row vector $[1, x, x^2, x^3, x^4, x^5]$ with the column

vector $[a_0, a_1, a_2, a_3, a_4, a_5]^T$. Work out the matrix version of this to give $[f(x_1), f(x_2), f(x_3), f(x_4), f(x_5), f(x_6)]^T$.)

6.3 | Eigenvalues and eigenvectors

Eigenvalues and eigenvectors can be computed using the function `eigen()`. For example,

```
> eigen(H3)
$values
[1] 1.408318927 0.122327066 0.002687340

$vectors
          [,1]         [,2]        [,3]
[1,]  0.8270449   0.5474484   0.1276593
[2,]  0.4598639  -0.5282902  -0.7137469
[3,]  0.3232984  -0.6490067   0.6886715
```

To see what this output means, let x_1 denote the first column of the `$vectors` output, i.e. $[0.827\ 0.459\ 0.323]^T$. This is the first eigenvector, and it corresponds to the eigenvalue 1.408. Thus,

$$H_3 x_1 = 1.408 x_1.$$

Denoting the second and third columns of `$vectors` by x_2 and x_3, we have

$$H_3 x_2 = 0.122 x_2,$$

and

$$H_3 x_3 = 0.00268 x_3.$$

Exercises

1 Calculate the matrix $H = X(X^T X)^{-1} X^T$, where X was as defined in Section 6.1.

2 Calculate the eigenvalues and eigenvectors of H.

3 Calculate the trace of the matrix H, and compare with the sum of the eigenvalues.

4 Calculate the determinant of the matrix H, and compare with the product of the eigenvalues.

5 Using the definition, verify that the columns of X and $I - H$ are eigenvectors of H.

6 Obtain the 6×6 Hilbert matrix, and compute its eigenvalues and eigenvectors. Compute the inverse of the matrix. Is there a relation between the eigenvalues of the inverse and the eigenvalues of the original matrix? Is there supposed to be a relationship?
Repeat the above analysis on the 7×7 Hilbert matrix.

6.4 | Advanced topics

6.4.1 The singular value decomposition of a matrix

The singular value decomposition of a square matrix A consists of three square matrices, U, D, and V. The matrix D is a diagonal matrix. The relation among these matrices is

$$A = UDV^T.$$

The matrices U and V are said to be *orthogonal*, which means that $U^{-1} = U^T$ and $V^{-1} = V^T$.

The singular value decomposition of a matrix is often used to obtain accurate solutions to linear systems of equations.

The elements of D are called the singular values of A. Note that $A^T A = V^{-1} D^2 V$. This is a "similarity transformation" which tells us that the squares of the singular values of A are the eigenvalues of $A^T A$.

The singular value decomposition can be obtained using the function svd(). For example, the singular value decomposition of the 3×3 Hilbert matrix H_3 is

```
> H3.svd <- svd(H3)
> H3.svd
$d
[1] 1.408318927 0.122327066 0.002687340
$u

            [,1]        [,2]        [,3]
[1,] -0.8270449  0.5474484  0.1276593
[2,] -0.4598639 -0.5282902 -0.7137469
[3,] -0.3232984 -0.6490067  0.6886715
$v

            [,1]        [,2]        [,3]
[1,] -0.8270449  0.5474484  0.1276593
[2,] -0.4598639 -0.5282902 -0.7137469
[3,] -0.3232984 -0.6490067  0.6886715
```

We can verify that these components can be multiplied in the appropriate way to reconstruct H_3:

```
> H3.svd$u %*% diag(H3.svd$d) %*% t(H3.svd$v)
          [,1]      [,2]      [,3]
[1,] 1.0000000 0.5000000 0.3333333
[2,] 0.5000000 0.3333333 0.2500000
[3,] 0.3333333 0.2500000 0.2000000
```

Because of the properties of the U, V and D matrices, the singular value decomposition provides a simple way to compute a matrix inverse.

For example, $H_3^{-1} = VD^{-1}U^T$ and can be recalculated as

```
> H3.svd$v %*% diag(1/H3.svd$d) %*% t(H3.svd$u)
      [,1] [,2] [,3]
[1,]    9  -36   30
[2,]  -36  192 -180
[3,]   30 -180  180
```

6.4.2 The Choleski decomposition of a positive definite matrix

If a matrix A is positive definite, it possesses a square root. In fact, there are usually several matrices B such that $B^2 = A$. The Choleski decomposition is similar, but the idea is to find an upper triangular matrix U such that $U^T U = A$. The function chol() accomplishes this task.

For example, we can compute the Choleski decomposition of the 3×3 Hilbert matrix.

```
> H3.chol <- chol(H3)
> H3.chol                       # This is U, the upper triangular matrix
      [,1]      [,2]      [,3]
[1,]    1 0.5000000 0.3333333
[2,]    0 0.2886751 0.2886751
[3,]    0 0.0000000 0.0745356
> crossprod(H3.chol, H3.chol)        # Multiplying U^T U to recover H3
          [,1]      [,2]      [,3]
[1,] 1.0000000 0.5000000 0.3333333
[2,] 0.5000000 0.3333333 0.2500000
[3,] 0.3333333 0.2500000 0.2000000
```

Once the Choleski decomposition of a matrix $A = U^T U$ has been obtained, we can compute the inverse of A using the fact that $A^{-1} = U^{-1}U^{-T}$ (where U^{-T} is a short way to write the transpose of U^{-1}). This computation is much more stable than direct calculation of A^{-1} by Gaussian elimination. The function chol2inv() does this calculation. For example, we can compute the inverse of H3 as

```
> chol2inv(H3.chol)
      [,1] [,2] [,3]
[1,]    9  -36   30
[2,]  -36  192 -180
[3,]   30 -180  180
```

Once the Choleski decomposition has been obtained, we can compute solutions to linear systems of the form

$$Ax = b.$$

If $A = U^T U$, then we see that $Ux = U^{-T}b$. Therefore, the solution x can be obtained in a two-step procedure:

1 Solve $U^T y = b$ for y. The solution will satisfy $y = U^{-T}b$.
2 Solve $Ux = y$.

The first system is lower triangular, so forward elimination can be used to solve it. The function `forwardsolve()` can be used for this. The second system is upper triangular, so back substitution using function `backsolve()` can be used.

For the problem $H_3 x = b$, where $b = [1\ 2\ 3]^T$, we can proceed as follows:

```
> b <- seq(1, 3)
> y <- forwardsolve(t(H3.chol), b)
> backsolve(H3.chol, y)                    # the solution x
[1]    27 -192   210
```

6.4.3 The QR decomposition of a matrix

Another way of decomposing a matrix A is via the QR decomposition

$$A = QR,$$

where Q is an orthogonal matrix, and R is an upper triangular matrix. This decomposition can be applied even if A is not square. Again, this decomposition can be used to obtain accurate solutions to linear systems of equations.

For example, suppose we want to solve

$$Ax = b$$

for x, given the $n \times n$ matrix A and n-vector b. If we compute the QR decomposition of A first, we can write

$$QRx = b.$$

Multiplying through by Q^T on the left gives

$$Rx = Q^T b.$$

This is an easier system to solve, because R is an upper triangular matrix. Note that $Q^T b$ is an easily calculated n-vector.

To obtain the decomposition, we use the `qr()` function. For example,

```
> H3.qr <- qr(H3)
> H3.qr
$qr
           [,1]        [,2]         [,3]
[1,] -1.1666667 -0.6428571 -0.450000000
[2,]  0.4285714 -0.1017143 -0.105337032
[3,]  0.2857143  0.7292564  0.003901372

$rank
[1] 3

$qraux
[1] 1.857142857 1.684240553 0.003901372

$pivot
[1] 1 2 3
```

```
attr(,"class")
[1] "qr"
```

The output is an object of class qr.

The functions qr.Q() and qr.R() can be applied to this object to obtain the explicit Q and R matrices. For our example, we have

```
> Q <- qr.Q(H3.qr)
> Q
            [,1]        [,2]        [,3]
[1,] -0.8571429  0.5016049  0.1170411
[2,] -0.4285714 -0.5684856 -0.7022469
[3,] -0.2857143 -0.6520864  0.7022469
> R <- qr.R(H3.qr)
> R
            [,1]        [,2]          [,3]
[1,] -1.166667 -0.6428571 -0.450000000
[2,]  0.000000 -0.1017143 -0.105337032
[3,]  0.000000  0.0000000  0.003901372
```

We can recover H_3 by multiplying Q by R:

```
> Q % * % R
            [,1]        [,2]        [,3]
[1,] 1.0000000 0.5000000 0.3333333
[2,] 0.5000000 0.3333333 0.2500000
[3,] 0.3333333 0.2500000 0.2000000
```

Again, the inverse of H_3 can be obtained from $R^{-1}Q^T$. Since R is upper triangular, this inverse can be computed quickly, in principle. In the following, we compute R^{-1} in a computationally inefficient way, simply to demonstrate that the decomposition can be used to get at the inverse of a matrix:

```
> qr.solve(R) % * % t(Q)
       [,1] [,2] [,3]
[1,]     9  -36   30
[2,]   -36  192 -180
[3,]    30 -180  180
```

6.4.4 The condition number of a matrix

The function kappa() can be used to compute the condition number of a given matrix (the ratio of the largest to smallest nonzero singular values). This gives an idea as to how bad certain numerical calculations will be when applied to the matrix. Large values of the condition number indicate poor numerical properties.

```
> kappa(H3)
[1] 646.2247
```

As this is a fairly large value, matrix inversion will not be very accurate.

6.4.5 Outer products

The function outer() is sometimes useful in statistical calculations. It can be used to perform an operation on all possible pairs of elements coming from two vectors.

A simple example involves computing all quotients among pairs of elements of the sequence running from 1 through 5:

```
> x1 <- seq(1, 5)
> outer(x1, x1, "/")      # or outer(x1, x1, function(x, y) x / y)
      [,1] [,2]      [,3] [,4] [,5]
[1,]    1  0.5 0.3333333 0.25  0.2
[2,]    2  1.0 0.6666667 0.50  0.4
[3,]    3  1.5 1.0000000 0.75  0.6
[4,]    4  2.0 1.3333333 1.00  0.8
[5,]    5  2.5 1.6666667 1.25  1.0
```

Replacing the division operation with the subtraction operator gives all pairwise differences:

```
> outer(x1, x1, "-")
     [,1] [,2] [,3] [,4] [,5]
[1,]    0   -1   -2   -3   -4
[2,]    1    0   -1   -2   -3
[3,]    2    1    0   -1   -2
[4,]    3    2    1    0   -1
[5,]    4    3    2    1    0
```

The third argument can be any function that takes two vector arguments. The second argument can differ from the first. For example,

```
> y <- seq(5, 10)
> outer(x1, y, "+")
     [,1] [,2] [,3] [,4] [,5] [,6]
[1,]    6    7    8    9   10   11
[2,]    7    8    9   10   11   12
[3,]    8    9   10   11   12   13
[4,]    9   10   11   12   13   14
[5,]   10   11   12   13   14   15
```

6.4.6 Kronecker products

The function kronecker() can be used to compute the Kronecker product of two matrices and other more general products. See the help() file for more information.

6.4.7 apply()

In statistical applications, it is sometimes necessary to apply the same function to each of the rows of a matrix, or to each of the columns. A for() loop could be used, but it is sometimes more efficient computationally to use the apply() function.

There are three arguments. The first specifies the matrix. The second specifies whether the operation is to be applied to rows (1) or columns (2). The third argument specifies the function that should be applied.

A simple example is to compute the sum of the rows of H_3:

```
> apply(H3, 1, sum)
[1] 1.8333333 1.0833333 0.7833333
```

Chapter exercises

1 Consider the following *circulant* matrix:

$$P = \begin{bmatrix} 0.1 & 0.2 & 0.3 & 0.4 \\ 0.4 & 0.1 & 0.2 & 0.3 \\ 0.3 & 0.4 & 0.1 & 0.2 \\ 0.2 & 0.3 & 0.4 & 0.1 \end{bmatrix}.$$

(a) P is an example of a stochastic matrix. Use the apply() function to verify that the row sums add to 1.

(b) Compute P^n for $n = 2, 3, 5, 10$. Is a pattern emerging?

(c) Find a nonnegative vector x whose elements sum to 1 and which satisfies

$$(I - P^T)x = 0.$$

Do you see any connection between P^{10} and x?

(d) Using a loop, generate a pseudorandom sequence of numbers y from the set $\{1, 2, 3, 4\}$ using the rules:

(i) set $y_1 \leftarrow 1$

(ii) for $j = 2, 3, \ldots, n$, set $y_j = k$ with probability $P_{y_{j-1}, k}$.

For example, y_2 would be assigned the value 1, with probability 0.1; 2, with probability 0.2; and so on. Choose n to be some large value like $10\,000$.

The resulting vector y is an example of a simulated Markov chain.

(e) Use the table() function to determine the relative frequency distribution of the four possible values in the y vector. Compare this distribution with the *stationary distribution* x calculated earlier.

2 Repeat the previous exercise using the matrix

$$P = \begin{bmatrix} 0.1 & 0.2 & 0.3 & 0.4 & 0.0 & 0.0 & 0.0 \\ 0.1 & 0.1 & 0.1 & 0.1 & 0.1 & 0.1 & 0.4 \\ 0.2 & 0.2 & 0.2 & 0.2 & 0.2 & 0.0 & 0.0 \\ 0.3 & 0.3 & 0.3 & 0.1 & 0.0 & 0.0 & 0.0 \\ 0.3 & 0.3 & 0.3 & 0.1 & 0.0 & 0.0 & 0.0 \\ 0.3 & 0.3 & 0.3 & 0.1 & 0.0 & 0.0 & 0.0 \\ 0.3 & 0.3 & 0.3 & 0.1 & 0.0 & 0.0 & 0.0 \end{bmatrix}.$$

3 An insurance company has four types of policies, which we will label A, B, C, and D.

- They have a total of 245 921 policies.
- The annual income from each policy is $10 for type A, $30 for type B, $50 for type C, and $100 for type D.
- The total annual income for all policies is $7 304 620.
- The claims on these policies arise at different rates. The expected number of type A claims is 0.1 claims per year, type B 0.15 claims per year, type C 0.03 claims per year, and type D 0.5 claims per year.
- The total expected number of claims for the company is 34 390.48 per year.
- The expected size of the claims is different for each policy type. For type A, it is $50, for type B it is $180, for type C it is $1500, and for type D it is $250.
- The expected total claim amount is $6 864 693. This is the sum over all policies of the expected size of claim times the expected number of claims in a year.

Use R to answer the following questions:

(a) Find the total number of each type of policy.
(b) Find the total income and total expected claim size for each type of policy.
(c) Assuming that claims arise in a Poisson process, and each claim amount follows a Gamma distribution with a shape parameter of 2 and the means listed above, use simulation to estimate the following:
  (i) The variance in the total claim amount.
  (ii) The probability that the total claim amount will exceed the total annual income from these policies.

  Write a function to do these calculations, and do it once for the overall company income and claims, and once for each of the four types of policy.

Numerical optimization

In many areas of statistics and applied mathematics one has to solve the following problem: given a function $f(\cdot)$, which value of x makes $f(x)$ as large or as small as possible?

For example, in financial modeling $f(x)$ might be the expected return from a portfolio, with x being a vector holding the amounts invested in each of a number of possible securities. There might be constraints on x (e.g. the amount to invest must be positive, the total amount invested must be fixed, etc.)

In statistical modeling, we may want to find a set of parameters for a model which minimize the expected prediction errors for the model. Here x would be the parameters and $f(\cdot)$ would be a measure of the prediction error.

Knowing how to do minimization is sufficient. If we want to maximize $f(x)$, we simply change the sign and minimize $-f(x)$. We call both operations "numerical optimization." Use of derivatives and simple algebra often lead to the solution of such problems, but not nearly always. Because of the wide range of possibilities for functions $f(\cdot)$ and parameters x, this is a rich area of computing.

7.1 | The golden section search method

The golden section search method is a simple way of finding the minimizer of a single-variable function which has a single minimum on the interval $[a, b]$.

Consider minimizing the function

$$f(x) = |x - 3.5| + (x - 2)^2$$

on the interval $[0, 5]$. This function is not differentiable at $x = 3.5$, so some care must be taken to find the minimizer. We can write an R function to evaluate $f(x)$ as follows:

```
> f <- function(x) {
+     abs(x - 3.5) + (x - 2)^2
+ }
```

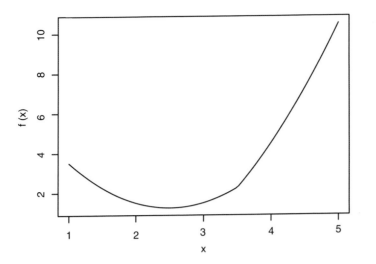

Fig. 7.1 The function $f(x) = |x - 3.5| + (x - 2)^2$.

To check that this function has a single minimum in the interval we use the `curve()` function to plot it:

```
> curve(f, from = 1, to = 5)
```

The curve is displayed in Figure 7.1, where we can see that the minimizer is located near $x = 2.5$.

The golden section search method is an iterative method, which may be outlined as follows:

1 Start with the interval $[a, b]$, known to contain the minimizer.
2 Repeatedly shrink it, finding smaller and smaller intervals $[a', b']$ which still contain the minimizer.
3 Stop when $b' - a'$ is small enough, i.e. when the interval length is less than a pre-set tolerance.

When the search stops, the midpoint of the final interval will serve as a good approximation to the true minimizer, with a maximum error of $(b' - a')/2$.

The shrinkage step 2 begins by evaluating the function at two points $x_1 < x_2$ in the interior of the interval $[a, b]$. (How the points are chosen will be described below.) Because we have assumed that there is a unique minimum, we know that if $f(x_1) > f(x_2)$, then the minimum must lie to the right of x_1, i.e. in the interval $[a', b'] = [x_1, b]$. If $f(x_1) < f(x_2)$, the minimum must lie in $[a', b'] = [a, x_2]$ (see Figure 7.2). (What if the values are exactly equal? We will consider that case later.) Then new values of $x_1, f(x_1), x_2$, and $f(x_2)$ are computed, and the method is repeated until the tolerance criterion is satisfied.

The choice of the points between a and b makes use of properties of the golden ratio $\phi = (\sqrt{5} + 1)/2$. The golden ratio (which we saw in Chapter 3 in the context of Fibonacci numbers) has a number of interesting algebraic properties. We make use of the fact that $1/\phi = \phi - 1$ and $1/\phi^2 = 1 - 1/\phi$ in the following. (Some authors call the value $\Phi = 1/\phi$ the "silver ratio," but we'll stick with ϕ in our formulas.)

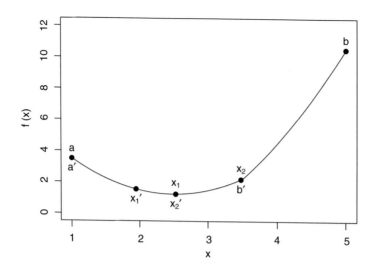

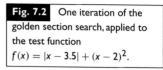

Fig. 7.2 One iteration of the golden section search, applied to the test function $f(x) = |x - 3.5| + (x - 2)^2$.

We locate the interior points at $x_1 = b - (b-a)/\phi$ and $x_2 = a + (b-a)/\phi$. The reason for this choice is as follows. After one iteration of the search, it is possible that we will throw away a and replace it with $a' = x_1$. Then the new value to use as x_1 will be

$$x_1' = b - (b - a')/\phi$$
$$= b - (b - x_1)/\phi$$
$$= b - (b - a)/\phi^2$$
$$= a + (b - a)/\phi$$
$$= x_2,$$

i.e. we can re-use a point we already have, we do not need a new calculation to find it, and we don't need a new evaluation of $f(x_1')$, we can re-use $f(x_2)$. Similarly, if we update to $b' = x_2$, then $x_2' = x_1$, and we can re-use that point.

We put this together into the following R function:

```
> golden <- function (f, a, b, tol = 0.0000001)
+ {
+       ratio <- 2 / (sqrt(5) + 1)
+       x1 <- b - ratio * (b - a)
+       x2 <- a + ratio * (b - a)
+
+       f1 <- f(x1)
+       f2 <- f(x2)
+
+       while(abs(b - a) > tol) {
+
+           if (f2 > f1) {
+               b <- x2
+               x2 <- x1
```

```
+              f2 <- f1
+              x1 <- b - ratio * (b - a)
+              f1 <- f(x1)
+          } else {
+              a <- x1
+              x1 <- x2
+              f1 <- f2
+              x2 <- a + ratio * (b - a)
+              f2 <- f(x2)
+          }
+      }
+      return((a + b) / 2)
+ }
```

We test and see that `golden()` works, at least on one function:

```
> golden(f, 1, 5)
[1] 2.5
```

Exercises

1 Apply the golden section minimization technique to the following functions:

  (a) $f(x) = |x - 3.5| + |x - 2| + |x - 1|$
  (b) $f(x) = |x - 3.2| + |x - 3.5| + |x - 2| + |x - 1|$.

  For the second function, check the graph to see that the minimizer is not unique. Show that the minimizer found by `golden()` depends on the initial interval supplied to the function.

2 For an odd number of data values $x_1, x_2, \ldots, x_n$, the minimizer of the function

$$f(x) = \sum_{i=1}^{n} |x - x_i|$$

  is the sample median of the data values. (Exercise 1(a) is an example of this.) Verify this result for the following data sets:

  (a) 3, 7, 9, 12, 15
  (b) 3, 7, 9, 12, 15, 18, 21.

  Describe, in words, what happens when the number of observations is even.

3 Write a function that would find the maximizer of a function using the golden section search.

7.2 | Newton–Raphson

If the function to be minimized has two continuous derivatives and we know how to evaluate them, we can make use of this information to give a faster algorithm than the golden section search.

We want to find a minimizer x^* of the function $f(x)$ in the interval $[a, b]$. Provided the minimizer is not at a or b, x^* will satisfy $f'(x^*) = 0$. This is a necessary condition for x^* to be a minimizer of $f(x)$, but it is not sufficient: we must check that x^* actually minimizes $f(x)$. Other solutions of $f'(x^*) = 0$ are maximizers and points of inflection. One sufficient condition to guarantee that our solution is a minimum is to check that $f''(x^*) > 0$.

Now, if we have a guess x_0 at a minimizer, we use the fact that $f''(x)$ is the slope of $f'(x)$ and approximate $f'(x)$ using a Taylor series approximation:

$$f'(x) \approx f'(x_0) + (x - x_0)f''(x_0).$$

Finding a zero of the right-hand side should give us an approximate solution to $f'(x^*) = 0$.

We implement this idea as follows, using the Newton–Raphson algorithm to approximate a solution to $f'(x^*) = 0$. Start with an initial guess x_0, and compute an improved guess using the solution

$$x_1 = x_0 - \frac{f'(x_0)}{f''(x_0)}.$$

This gives a new guess at the minimizer. Then use x_1 in place of x_0, to obtain a new update x_2. Continue with iterations of the form

$$x_{n+1} = x_n - \frac{f'(x_n)}{f''(x_n)}.$$

This iteration stops when $f'(x_n)$ is close enough to 0. Usually, we set a tolerance ε and stop when $|f'(x_n)| < \varepsilon$.

It can be shown that the Newton–Raphson method is guaranteed to converge to a local minimizer, provided the starting value x_0 is close enough to the minimizer. As with other numerical optimization techniques, where there are multiple minimizers, Newton–Raphson won't necessarily find the best one. However, when $f''(x) > 0$ everywhere, there will be only one minimizer.

In actual practice, implementation of Newton–Raphson can be tricky. We may have $f''(x_n) = 0$, in which case the function looks locally like a straight line, with no solution to the Taylor series approximation to $f'(x^*) = 0$. In this case a simple strategy is to move a small step in the direction which decreases the function value, based only on $f'(x_n)$.

In other cases where x_n is too far from the true minimizer, the Taylor approximation may be so inaccurate that $f(x_{n+1})$ is actually larger than $f(x_n)$. When this happens one may replace x_{n+1} with $(x_{n+1} + x_n)/2$ (or some other value between x_n and x_{n+1}) in the hope that a smaller step will produce better results.

Finally, there is always the possibility that the code to calculate $f'(x)$ or $f''(x)$ may contain bugs: it is usually worthwhile to do careful checks to make sure this is not the case.

Example 7.1

We wish to find the minimizer of $f(x) = e^{-x} + x^4$. By inspection, we can guess that the minimizer is somewhere to the right of zero, because e^{-x} is a decreasing function, and x^4 has a minimum at zero. We start by plotting the function to find an initial guess (Figure 7.3):

```
> f <- function(x) exp(-x) + x^4
> curve(f, from=-1, to=4)
```

From the figure, we can see that the minimizer is somewhere near $x_0 = 0.5$; we will use that as our starting value. Because of the difficulties mentioned above, we will not attempt to write a general Newton–Raphson implementation. Instead, we will simply evaluate several updates to see whether it converges or not.

```
> f <- function(x) exp(-x) + x^4
> fprime <- function(x) -exp(-x) + 4 * x^3
> fprimeprime <- function(x) exp(-x) + 12 * x^2
> x <- c(0.5, rep(NA, 6))
> fval <- rep(NA, 7)
> fprimeval <- rep(NA, 7)
> fprimeprimeval <- rep(NA, 7)
> for (i in 1:6) {
+       fval[i] <- f(x[i])
+       fprimeval[i] <- fprime(x[i])
+       fprimeprimeval[i] <- fprimeprime(x[i])
+       x[i + 1] <- x[i] - fprimeval[i] / fprimeprimeval[i]
+ }
> data.frame(x, fval, fprimeval, fprimeprimeval)
          x        fval      fprimeval fprimeprimeval
1 0.5000000 0.6690307 -1.065307e-01       3.606531
2 0.5295383 0.6675070  5.076129e-03       3.953806
3 0.5282544 0.6675038  9.980020e-06       3.938266
4 0.5282519 0.6675038  3.881429e-11       3.938235
5 0.5282519 0.6675038  0.000000e+00       3.938235
6 0.5282519 0.6675038  0.000000e+00       3.938235
7 0.5282519        NA            NA             NA
```

We see that convergence was very rapid, with the derivative numerically equal to zero by the fourth update. The second derivative is positive there, confirming that this is a local minimum. In fact, since $f''(x) = e^{-x} + 12x^2$, the second derivative is positive everywhere, and we can be sure that this is a global minimum.

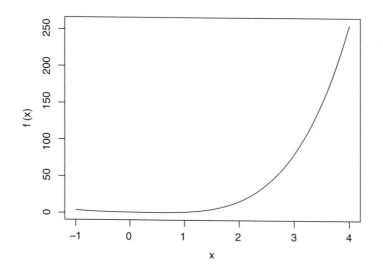

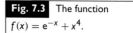

Fig. 7.3 The function $f(x) = e^{-x} + x^4$.

7.3 | The Nelder–Mead simplex method

In the previous sections, we have talked about two different methods for optimizing a function of one variable. However, when a function depends on multiple inputs, optimization becomes much harder. It is hard even to visualize the function once it depends on more than two inputs.

The Nelder–Mead simplex algorithm is one method for optimization of a function of several variables. In p dimensions, it starts with $p + 1$ points $x_1, \ldots, x_{p+1}$, arranged so that when considered as vertices of a p-dimensional solid (a "simplex"), they enclose a nonzero volume. For example, in two dimensions the three points would not be allowed to all lie on one line so they would form a triangle, and in three dimensions the four points would form a proper tetrahedron.

The points are labeled in order from smallest to largest values of $f(x_i)$, so that $f(x_1) \leq f(x_2) \leq \cdots \leq f(x_{p+1})$. The idea is that to minimize $f(x)$, we would like to drop x_{p+1} and replace it with a point that gives a smaller value. We do this by calculating several proposed points z_i from the existing points. There are four kinds of proposals, illustrated in Figure 7.4 in two dimensions. The first three refer to the midpoint of $x_1, \ldots, x_p$ which we calculate as $x_{\mathrm{mid}} = (x_1 + \cdots + x_p)/p$.

1 Reflection: reflect x_{p+1} through x_{mid} to z_1.
2 Reflection and expansion: reflect x_{p+1} through x_{mid}, and double its distance, giving z_2.
3 Contraction 1: contract x_{p+1} halfway towards x_{mid} to give z_3.
4 Contraction 2: contract all points halfway towards x_1, giving $z_4, \ldots, z_{p+3}$.

We consider each of these choices of simplex in order, based on the values of $f(z_i)$. It is helpful to consider the line shown in Figure 7.5 as you

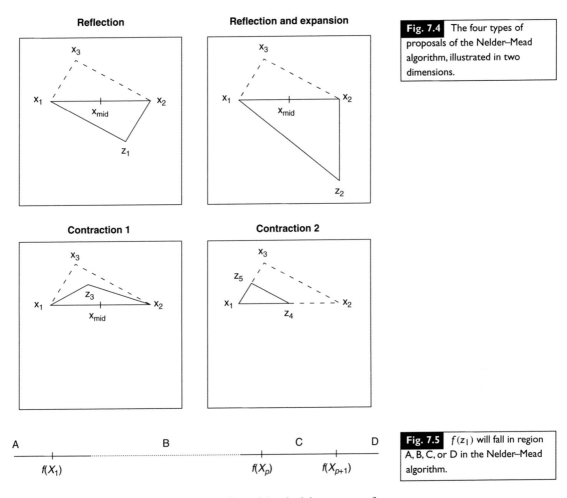

Fig. 7.4 The four types of proposals of the Nelder–Mead algorithm, illustrated in two dimensions.

Fig. 7.5 $f(z_1)$ will fall in region A, B, C, or D in the Nelder–Mead algorithm.

read through the following pseudocode outline of the decision process for one update of the simplex:

```
Initialization:
    Place the initial points in a matrix x, so that point i is in
      x[i,]
    For i in 1:(p + 1) calculate f(x[i,])
    Relabel the points so that
      f(x[1,]) <= f(x[2,]) <= ... <= f(x[p + 1,])
    Calculate the midpoint xmid = (x[1,] + x[2,] + ... + x[p,]) / p

Trials:
    Calculate z1 by reflection:  z1 <- xmid - (x[p + 1,] - xmid)
    If f(z1) < f(x[1,]) {                      # Region A
        Calculate z2 by reflection and expansion:
          z2 <- xmid - 2 * (x[p + 1,] - xmid)
        If f(z2) < f(z1) return(z2)
        else return(z1)
    } else {
```

```
            If f(z1) < f(x[p,]) return(z1)          # Region B
            If f(z1) < f(x[p + 1,]) {
                Swap z1 with x[p + 1,]              # Region C
            }
        }
    }

    At this point we know f(z1) is in region D.

    Try contraction 1, giving z3.
    If f(z3) < f(x[p + 1,]) return(z3)              # Region A, B, or C

    At this point nothing has worked, so we use contraction 2 to move
        everything towards x[1,]
```

Example 7.2
In this example we try to minimize the function

```
> f <- function(x, y) ((x - y)^2 + (x - 2)^2 + (y - 3)^4) / 10
```

using the Nelder–Mead algorithm. We start by drawing a contour plot of
the function, in order to get approximate starting values. After some exper-
imentation, we obtain the plot shown in Figure 7.6 using the following
code:

```
> x <- seq(0, 5, len=20)
> y <- seq(0, 5, len=20)
> z <- outer(x, y, f)
> contour(x, y, z)
```

We implemented the Nelder–Mead update algorithm in an R function
with header neldermead(x, f), where x is our matrix in the pseudocode, and f is the function. The output of neldermead(x, f) is an
updated copy of the matrix x. The following log shows the output of nine
Nelder–Mead updates. Figure 7.7 shows the steps the algorithm took in this
demonstration.

```
> x <- matrix(c(0, 0, 2, 0, 2, 0), 3, 2)
> polygon(x)
> for (i in 1:9) {
+    cat(i, ":") +   x <- neldermead(x,f) +   polygon(x) +
text(rbind(apply(x, 2, mean)), labels=i) + }
1 :Accepted reflection, f(z1)= 3.3
2 :Swap z1 and x3
Accepted contraction 1, f(z3)= 3.25
3 :Accepted reflection and expansion, f(z2)= 0.31875
4 :Accepted reflection, f(z1)= 0.21875
5 :Accepted contraction 1, f(z3)= 0.21875
6 :Accepted contraction 1, f(z3)= 0.1
```

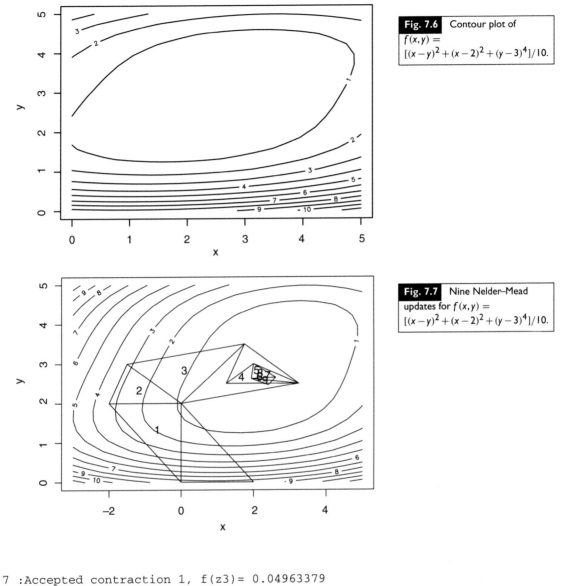

Fig. 7.6 Contour plot of
$f(x,y) =$
$[(x-y)^2 + (x-2)^2 + (y-3)^4]/10$.

Fig. 7.7 Nine Nelder–Mead
updates for $f(x,y) =$
$[(x-y)^2 + (x-2)^2 + (y-3)^4]/10$.

```
7 :Accepted contraction 1, f(z3)= 0.04963379
8 :Accepted contraction 1, f(z3)= 0.03874979
9 :Swap z1 and x3
Accepted contraction 1, f(z3)= 0.02552485
> x
          [,1]      [,2]
[1,] 2.609375 2.656250
[2,] 1.937500 2.625000
[3,] 2.410156 2.460938
```

At the end of these nine steps, we see that x should be around 1.9–2.6, and y should be around 2.4–2.7. A further 50 updates narrows these down to the true minimum at $(x,y) = (2.25, 2.5)$.

7.4 | Built-in functions

There are several general purpose optimization functions in R.

For one-dimensional optimization, the optimize() function performs a variation on the golden section search we described earlier. There are also multi-dimensional optimizers. The first of these is the optim() function. optim() is a general purpose wrapper for several different optimization methods, including Nelder–Mead, variations on Newton–Raphson, and others that we haven't discussed.

Syntax
```
optim(par, fn, ...)
```

The par parameter to optim() gives starting values for the parameters. Besides telling optim() where to begin, these indicate how many parameters will vary in its calls to fn, the second parameter. fn is an R function which evaluates the function to be minimized. Its first argument should be a vector of the same length as par; optim() will call it repeatedly, varying the value of this parameter, in order to find the minimum. It should return a scalar value. The optim() function has a number of optional parameters described on its help page. Besides those, the optional parameters in the . . . list could include additional parameters to pass to fn.

There are other functions in R for general function optimization: nlm() and nlminb(). In most cases optim() is preferred because it offers more flexibility, but there may be instances where one of the others performs better. The constrOptim() function is aimed at cases where there are linear inequalities expressing constraints on the parameters.

Exercises

1 Use the optimize() function to minimize the following functions:
   (a) $f(x) = |x - 3.5| + |x - 2| + |x - 1|$
   (b) $f(x) = |x - 3.2| + |x - 3.5| + |x - 2| + |x - 1|$.
2 Use nlm() and optim() to minimize the function

$$f(a, b) = (a - 1) + 3.2/b + 3\log(\Gamma(a)) + 3a\log(b).$$

Note that $\Gamma(a)$ is the gamma function which can be evaluated in R using gamma(a).
3 Re-do the previous exercise using nlminb(), noting that a and b should be restricted to being nonnegative.

7.5 | Linear programming

We often need to minimize (or maximize) a function subject to constraints. When the function is linear and the constraints can be expressed as linear equations or inequalities, the problem is called a *linear programming* problem.

The so-called standard form for the minimization problem in linear programming is

$$\min_{x_1, x_2, \ldots, x_k} C(x) = c_1 x_1 + \cdots + c_k x_k,$$

subject to the *constraints*

$$a_{11}x_1 + \cdots + a_{1k}x_k \geq b_1$$
$$a_{21}x_1 + \cdots + a_{2k}x_k \geq b_2$$
$$\cdots$$
$$a_{m1}x_1 + \cdots + a_{mk}x_k \geq b_m,$$

and the *nonnegativity conditions* $x_1 \geq 0, \ldots, x_k \geq 0$.

The idea is to find values of the *decision variables* $x_1, x_2, \ldots, x_n$ which minimize the *objective function* $C(x)$, subject to the constraints and nonnegativity conditions.

Example 7.3

A company has developed two procedures for reducing sulfur dioxide and carbon dioxide emissions from its factory. The first procedure reduces equal amounts of each gas at a per unit cost of \$5. The second procedure reduces the same amount of sulfur dioxide as the first method, but reduces twice as much carbon dioxide gas; the per unit cost of this method is \$8.

The company is required to reduce sulfur dioxide emissions by 2 million units and carbon dioxide emissions by 3 million units. What combination of the two emission procedures will meet this requirement at minimum cost?

Let x_1 denote the amount of the first procedure to be used, and let x_2 denote the amount of the second procedure to be used. For convenience, we will let these amounts be expressed in millions of units.

Then the cost (in millions of dollars) can be expressed as

$$C = 5x_1 + 8x_2.$$

Since both methods reduce sulfur dioxide emissions at the same rate, the number of units of sulfur dioxide reduced will then be

$$x_1 + x_2.$$

Noting that there is a requirement to reduce the sulfur dioxide amount by 2 million units, we have the constraint

$$x_1 + x_2 \geq 2.$$

The carbon dioxide reduction requirement is 3 million units, and the second method reduces carbon dioxide twice as fast as the first method, so we have the second constraint

$$x_1 + 2x_2 \geq 3.$$

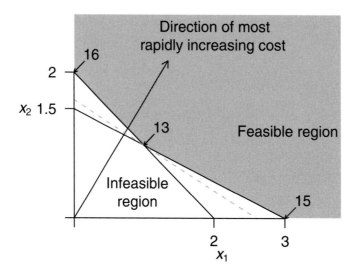

Fig. 7.8 A graphical interpretation of the pollution emission linear programming example. The grey region corresponds to values of x_1 and x_2 which satisfy all of the constraints. The dashed grey line corresponds to values of x_1 and x_2 which give the minimum cost (13); note that this line intersects the feasible region at exactly one point – the optimal solution to the problem (1, 1).

Finally, we note that x_1 and x_2 must be nonnegative, since we cannot use negative amounts of either procedure. Thus, we obtain the linear programming problem:

$$\min C = 5x_1 + 8x_2,$$

subject to the constraints

$$x_1 + x_2 \geq 2$$

$$x_1 + 2x_2 \geq 3,$$

and

$$x_1, x_2 \geq 0.$$

These relations are graphed in Figure 7.8. The region shaded in grey is the *feasible region*; this is the set of all possible (x_1, x_2) combinations which satisfy the constraints. The unshaded area contains those combinations of values where the constraints are violated.

The gradient of the function $C(x)$ is (5, 8), so this vector gives the direction of most rapid increase for that function. The level sets or contours of this function are perpendicular to this vector. One of the level sets is indicated as a dashed line in Figure 7.8. The solution of the minimization problem lies at the intersection of the first contour which intersects the feasible region. If this happens at a single point, we have a *unique* minimizer. In this example, this intersection is located at the point (1, 1).

It can be shown that the only possible minimizers for such linear programming problems must be at the intersections of the constraint boundaries, as in the above example. The points of intersection of the constraints are called *basic solutions*. If these intersection points lie in the feasible region, they are called *basic feasible solutions*. If there is at least one basic feasible solution, then one of them will be an *optimal solution*. In the above example, the point $(1, 1)$ is the optimal solution.

7.5.1 Solving linear programming problems in R

There is more than one linear programming function available in R, but we believe the `lp()` function in the `lpSolve` package may be the most stable version currently available. It is based on the *revised simplex method*; this method intelligently tests a number of extreme points of the feasible region to see whether they are optimal.

The `lp()` function has a number of parameters; the following are needed to solve minimization problems like the one in the earlier example:

- `objective.in` – the vector of coefficients of the objective function
- `const.mat` – a matrix containing the coefficients of the decision variables in the left-hand side of the constraints; each row corresponds to a constraint
- `const.dir` – a character vector indicating the direction of the constraint inequalities; some of the possible entries are `>=`, `==` and `<=`
- `const.rhs` – a vector containing the constants given on the right-hand side of the constraints.

Example 7.4
To solve the minimization problem set out in Example 7.3, type

```
> library(lpSolve)
> eg.lp <- lp(objective.in=c(5, 8), const.mat=matrix(c(1, 1, 1, 2),
+              nrow=2), const.rhs=c(2, 3), const.dir=c(">=", ">="))
> eg.lp
Success: the objective function is 13
> eg.lp$solution
[1] 1 1
```

The output tells us that the minimizer is at $x_1 = 1, x_2 = 1$, and the minimum value of the objective function is 13.

7.5.2 Maximization and other kinds of constraints

The `lp()` function can handle maximization problems with the use of the `direction="max"` parameter. Furthermore, the `const.dir` parameter allows for different types of inequalities.

Example 7.5
We will solve the problem:

$$\max C = 5x_1 + 8x_2,$$

subject to the constraints

$$x_1 + x_2 \leq 2$$
$$x_1 + 2x_2 = 3,$$

and

$$x_1, x_2 \geq 0.$$

In R, this can be coded as

```
> eg.lp <- lp(objective.in=c(5, 8),
+                  const.mat=matrix(c(1, 1, 1, 2), nrow=2),
+                  const.rhs=c(2, 3),
+                  const.dir=c("<=", "="), direction="max")
> eg.lp$solution
[1] 1 1
```

The solution is $(1, 1)$, giving a maximum value of 13.

7.5.3 Special situations
Multiple optima

It sometimes happens that there are multiple solutions for a linear programming problem.

Example 7.6

A slight modification of the pollution emission example (Example 7.3) is

$$\min C = 4x_1 + 8x_2,$$

subject to the constraints

$$x_1 + x_2 \geq 2$$

$$x_1 + 2x_2 \geq 3,$$

and

$$x_1, x_2 \geq 0.$$

This problem has a solution at $(1, 1)$ as well as at $(3, 0)$. All points on the line joining these two points are solutions as well. Figure 7.9 shows this graphically.

The `lp()` function does not alert the user to the existence of multiple minima. In fact, the output from this function for the modified pollution emission example is the solution $x_1 = 3, x_2 = 0$.

Degeneracy

For a problem with m decision variables, degeneracy arises when more than m constraint boundaries intersect at a single point. This situation is quite rare, but it has potential to cause difficulties for the simplex method, so it is important to be aware of this condition. In very rare circumstances,

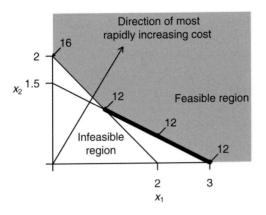

Fig. 7.9 A plot of the gradient of the objective function and the constraint boundaries for Example 7.6. The points on the heavy black segment are all optimal for this problem.

degeneracy can prevent the method from converging to the optimal solution; most of the time, however, there is little to worry about.

Example 7.7
The following problem has a point of degeneracy which is not at the optimum; however, the lp() function still finds the optimum without difficulty.

$$\min C = 3x_1 + x_2,$$

subject to the constraints

$$x_1 + x_2 \geq 2$$

$$x_1 + 2x_2 \geq 3$$

$$x_1 + 3x_2 \geq 4$$

$$4x_1 + x_2 \geq 4,$$

and

$$x_1, x_2 \geq 0.$$

The constraint boundaries are plotted in Figure 7.10.
   This problem can be solved easily:

```
> degen.lp <- lp(objective.in=c(3, 1),
+                const.mat=matrix(c(1, 1, 1, 4, 1, 2, 3, 1), nrow=4),
+                const.rhs=c(2, 3, 4, 4), const.dir=rep(">=", 4))
> degen.lp

Success: the objective function is 3.333333
> degen.lp$solution
[1] 0.6666667 1.3333333
```

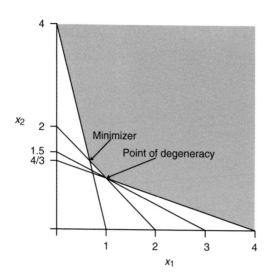

Fig. 7.10 A plot of four constraint boundaries, one of which is redundant, leading to degeneracy. The feasible region is shaded.

Infeasibility

Infeasibility is a more common problem. When the constraints cannot simultaneously be satisfied there is no feasible region. Then no feasible solution exists.

Example 7.8

In the following example, it is obvious that the constraints cannot simultaneously be satisfied.

$$\min C = 5x_1 + 8x_2,$$

subject to the constraints

$$x_1 + x_2 \geq 2$$
$$x_1 + x_2 \leq 1,$$

and

$$x_1, x_2 \geq 0.$$

Here is the output from the `lp()` function:

```
> eg.lp <- lp(objective.in=c(5, 8),
+              const.mat=matrix(c(1, 1, 1, 1), nrow=2),
+              const.rhs=c(2, 1), const.dir=c(">=", "<="))
> eg.lp
Error: no feasible solution found
```

Unboundedness

In rare instances, the constraints and objective function give rise to an unbounded solution.

Example 7.9
A trivial example of unboundedness arises when solving the problem

$$\max C = 5x_1 + 8x_2,$$

subject to the constraints

$$x_1 + x_2 \geq 2$$
$$x_1 + 2x_2 \geq 3,$$

and

$$x_1, x_2 \geq 0.$$

The feasible region for this problem is the same as for Example 7.3 and is plotted in Figure 7.8. However, instead of trying to minimize the objective function, we are now maximizing, so we follow the direction of increasing the objective function this time. We can make the objective function as large as we wish, by taking x_1 and x_2 arbitrarily large.

Here is what happens when `lp()` is applied to this problem:

```
> eg.lp <- lp(objective.in=c(5, 8),
+                 const.mat=matrix(c(1, 1, 1, 2), nrow=2),
+                 const.rhs=c(2, 3), const.dir=c(">=", ">="),
+                 direction="max")
> eg.lp
Error: status 3
```

The condition of unboundedness will most often arise when constraints and/or the objective function have not been formulated correctly.

7.5.4 Unrestricted variables
Sometimes a decision variable is not restricted to being nonnegative. The `lp()` function is not set up to handle this case directly. However, a simple device gets around this difficulty.

If x is unrestricted in sign, then x can be written as $x_1 - x_2$, where $x_1 \geq 0$ and $x_2 \geq 0$. This means that every unrestricted variable in a linear programming problem can be replaced by the difference of two nonnegative variables.

Example 7.10
We will solve the problem:

$$\min C = x_1 + 10x_2,$$

subject to the constraints

$$x_1 + x_2 \geq 2$$
$$x_1 - x_2 \leq 3,$$

and

$$x_1 \geq 0.$$

Noting that x_2 is unrestricted in sign, we set $x_2 = x_3 - x_4$ for nonnegative x_3 and x_4. Plugging these new variables into the problem gives

$$\min C = x_1 + 10x_3 - 10x_4,$$

subject to the constraints

$$x_1 + x_3 - x_4 \geq 2$$
$$x_1 - x_3 + x_4 \leq 3,$$

and

$$x_1 \geq 0, x_3 \geq 0, x_4 \geq 0.$$

Converting this to R code, we have

```
> unres.lp <- lp(objective.in=c(1, 10, -10),
+        const.mat=matrix(c(1, 1, 1, -1, -1, 1), nrow=2),
+        const.rhs=c(2, 3), const.dir=c(">=", "<="))
> unres.lp
Success: the objective function is -2.5
> unres.lp$solution
[1] 2.5 0.0 0.5
```

The solution is given by $x_1 = 2.5$ and $x_2 = x_3 - x_4 = -0.5$.

7.5.5 Integer programming

Decision variables are often restricted to be integers. For example, we might want to minimize the cost of shipping a product by using one, two, or three different trucks. It is not possible to use a fractional number of trucks, so the number of trucks must be integer-valued.

Problems involving integer-valued decision variables are called *integer programming* problems. Simple rounding of a non-integer solution to the nearest integer is *not* good practice; the result of such rounding can be a solution which is quite far from the optimal solution.

The `lp()` function has a facility to handle integer-valued variables using a technique called the *branch and bound algorithm*. The `int.vec` argument can be used to indicate which variables have integer values.

Example 7.11
Find nonnegative x_1, x_2, x_3, and x_4 to minimize

$$C(x) = 2x_1 + 3x_2 + 4x_3 - x_4,$$

subject to the constraints

$$x_1 + 2x_2 \geq 9$$
$$3x_2 + x_3 \geq 9,$$

and

$$x_2 + x_4 \leq 10.$$

Furthermore, x_2 and x_4 can only take integer values. To set up and solve this problem in R, type

```
> integ.lp <- lp(objective.in=c(2, 3, 4, -1),
+     const.mat=matrix(c(1, 0, 0, 2, 3, 1, 0, 1, 0, 0, 0, 1), nrow=3),
+     const.dir=c(">=", ">=", "<="), const.rhs=c(9, 9, 10),
+     int.vec=c(2, 4))
> integ.lp
Success: the objective function is 8
> integ.lp$solution
[1] 1 4 0 6
```

Thus, the best solution when x_2 and x_4 are integer-valued is $x_1 = 1, x_2 = 4$, $x_3 = 0$, and $x_4 = 6$.

Here is what happens when the integer variables are ignored:

```
> wrong.lp <- lp(objective.in=c(2, 3, 4, -1),
+     const.mat=matrix(c(1, 0, 0, 2, 3, 1, 0, 1, 0, 0, 0, 1), nrow=3),
+     const.dir=c(">=", ">=", "<="), const.rhs=c(9, 9, 10))
> wrong.lp
Success: the objective function is 8
> wrong.lp$solution
[1] 0.0 4.5 0.0 5.5
```

Rounding the solution to the nearest integer will lead to a violation of the first constraint (if x_2 is taken to be 4) or to a minimum value of the objective function that is larger than 8 (if $x_2 = 5$).

7.5.6 Alternatives to lp()

The lp() function provides an interface to code written in C. There is another function in the linprog package called solveLP() which is written entirely in R; this latter function solves large problems much more slowly than the lp() function, but it provides more detailed output. We note also the function simplex() in the boot package.

It should also be noted that, for very large problems, the simplex method might not converge quickly enough; better procedures, called *interior point methods*, have been discovered recently, and are implemented in other programming languages, but not yet in R.

7.5.7 Quadratic programming

Linear programming problems are a special case of optimization problems in which a possibly nonlinear function is minimized subject to constraints. Such problems are typically more difficult to solve and are beyond the scope of this text; an exception is the case where the objective function is quadratic and the constraints are linear. This is a problem in *quadratic programming*.

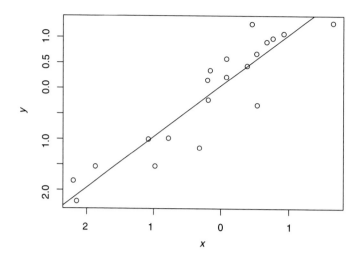

Fig. 7.11 A scatterplot of the 20 observations with a line of slope 1 and intercept 0.05 overlaid.

A quadratic programming problem with k constraints is often of the form

$$\min_{\beta} \frac{1}{2}\beta^T D\beta - d^T\beta,$$

subject to constraints $A^T\beta \geq b$. Here β is a vector of p unknowns, D is a positive definite $p \times p$ matrix, d is vector of length p, A is a $p \times k$ matrix, and b is a vector of length k.

Example 7.12
Consider the following 20 pairs of observations on the variables x and y. A scatterplot is displayed in Figure 7.11.

```
> x <- c(0.45,   0.08, -1.08,   0.92,   1.65,   0.53, 0.52, -2.15, -2.20,
+            -0.32, -1.87, -0.16, -0.19, -0.98, -0.20, 0.67,  0.08,  0.38,
+             0.76, -0.78)
> y <- c(1.26,   0.58, -1.00,   1.07,   1.28, -0.33, 0.68, -2.22, -1.82,
+            -1.17, -1.54,   0.35, -0.23, -1.53,   0.16, 0.91,  0.22,  0.44,
+             0.98, -0.98)
```

Our problem is to pass a line of "best-fit" through these data. We seek a line of the form

$$y = \beta_0 + \beta_1 x,$$

where β_0 is the y-intercept and β_1 is the slope. However, we have additional background information about these data that indicate that the slope β_1 of the required line is at least 1.

The line we want is the one that minimizes the sum of the squared vertical distances between the observed points and the line itself:

$$\min_{\beta_0, \beta_1} \sum_{i=1}^{20} (y_i - \beta_0 - \beta_1 x_i)^2.$$

Our extra information about the slope tells us that this minimization is subject to the constraint $\beta_1 \geq 1$.

This is an example of a *restricted least-squares* problem and is equivalent to

$$\min_{\beta} \ \beta^T X^T X \beta - 2y^T X \beta,$$

subject to

$$A\beta \geq b,$$

where $A = [0 \ 1]$, $\beta = [\beta_0 \ \beta_1]^T$, y is a column vector consisting of the 20 y measurements, and X is a matrix consisting of two columns, where the first column contains only 1's and the second column contains the 20 x observations:

$$X = \begin{bmatrix} 1 & x_1 \\ 1 & x_2 \\ \cdots & \cdots \\ 1 & x_n \end{bmatrix} = \begin{bmatrix} 1 & 0.45 \\ 1 & 0.08 \\ \cdots & \cdots \\ 1 & -0.78 \end{bmatrix}.$$

We then have

$$X^T X = \begin{bmatrix} n & \sum_{i=1}^n x_i \\ \sum_{i=1}^n x_i & \sum_{i=1}^n x_i^2 \end{bmatrix} = \begin{bmatrix} 20 & -3.89 \\ -3.89 & 21.4 \end{bmatrix},$$

$$y^T X = \begin{bmatrix} \sum_{i=1}^n y_i & \sum_{i=1}^n x_i y_i \end{bmatrix} = [-2.89 \ 20.7585].$$

This is a quadratic programming problem with $D = X^T X$ and $d = y^T X$.

Linear programming methods have been adapted to handle quadratic programming problems. The `solve.QP()` function is in the `quadprog` package. It solves minimization problems, and the following are parameters which are required:

- `Dmat` – a matrix containing the elements of the matrix (D) of the quadratic form in the objective function
- `dvec` – a vector containing the coefficients of the decision variables in the objective function
- `Amat` – a matrix containing the coefficients of the decision variables in the constraints; each row of the matrix corresponds to a constraint
- `bvec` – a vector containing the constants given on the right-hand side of the constraints
- `mvec` – a number indicating the number of equality constraints. By default, this is 0. If it is not 0, the equality constraints should be listed ahead of the inequality constraints.

The output from this function is a list whose first two elements are the vector that minimizes the function and the minimum value of the function.

Example 7.13

For the restricted least squares problem of Example 7.12, we must first set up the matrices D and A as well as the vectors b and d. Here, $D = X^T X$ and $d = X^T y$.

```
> library(quadprog)
> X <- cbind(rep(1, 20), x)
> XX <- t(X) %*% X
> Xy <- t(X) %*% y
> A <- matrix(c(0, 1), ncol=1)
> b <- 1
> solve.QP(Dmat=XX, dvec=Xy, Amat=A, bvec=b)
$solution
[1] 0.05 1.00

$value
[1] -10.08095
$unconstrainted.solution
[1] 0.04574141 0.97810494

$iterations
[1] 2 0

$iact
[1] 1
```

From the output, we see that the required line is

$$\hat{y} = 0.05 + x.$$

The rest of the output is indicating that the constraint is *active*. If the unconstrained problem had yielded a slope larger than 1, the constraint would have been *inactive*, and the solution to the unconstrained problem would be the same as the solution to the constrained problem.

Note that the decision variables in the above example were restricted in sign. If needed, nonnegativity conditions must be explicitly set when using the `solve.QP()` function. Also, it should be noted that inequality constraints are all of the form >=. If your problem contains some inequality constraints with <=, then the constraints should be multiplied through by -1 to convert them to the required form.

It should be noted that there are more efficient ways to solve restricted least squares problems in other computing environments. The matrix D in the preceding example is a diagonal matrix, and this special structure can be used to reduce the computational burden. The following example involves a full matrix. This example also places a restriction on the sign of the decision variables.

Example 7.14
Quadratic programming can be applied to the problem of finding an optimal portfolio for an investor who is choosing how much money to invest in each of a set of n stocks. A simple model for this problem boils down to maximizing

$$x^T \beta - \frac{k}{2} \beta^T D \beta,$$

subject to the constraints $\sum_{i=1}^{n} \beta_i = 1$ and $\beta_i \geq 0$ for $i = 1, \ldots, n$.

The ith component of the β vector represents the fraction of the investor's fortune that should be invested in the ith stock. Note that each element of this vector must be nonnegative, since the investor cannot allocate a negative fraction of her portfolio to a stock.[1] The vector x contains the average daily *returns* for each stock; the daily return value for a stock is the difference in closing price for the stock from one day to the next. Therefore, $x^T \beta$ represents the average daily return for the investor.

Most investors do not want to take large risks; the second term in the objective function takes this fact into account. The factor k quantifies the investor's tolerance for risk. If the investor's goal is purely to maximize the average daily return without regard for the risk, then $k = 0$. The value of k is larger for an investor who is concerned about taking risks. The D matrix quantifies the underlying variability in the returns; it is called a *covariance* matrix. The diagonal elements of the D matrix are the variances of the returns for each of the stocks. An off-diagonal element (i, j) is the covariance between returns of the ith and jth stocks; this is a simple measure of relation between the two returns.

For a specific example, we consider three stocks and set $k = 4$ and

$$D = \begin{bmatrix} 0.010 & 0.002 & 0.002 \\ 0.002 & 0.010 & 0.002 \\ 0.002 & 0.002 & 0.010 \end{bmatrix}.$$

We assume the mean daily returns for the three stocks are 0.002, 0.005, and 0.01, respectively, so $x^T = [0.002 \ 0.005 \ 0.01]$.

The requirement that $\beta_1 + \beta_2 + \beta_3 = 1$ and the nonnegativity restrictions on the β variables can be written as

$$\begin{bmatrix} 1 & 1 & 1 \\ 1 & 0 & 0 \\ 0 & 1 & 0 \\ 0 & 0 & 1 \end{bmatrix} \begin{bmatrix} \beta_1 \\ \beta_2 \\ \beta_3 \end{bmatrix} \begin{matrix} = \\ \geq \\ \geq \\ \geq \end{matrix} \begin{bmatrix} 1 \\ 0 \\ 0 \\ 0 \end{bmatrix}.$$

Therefore, we take

$$A^T = \begin{bmatrix} 1 & 1 & 1 \\ 1 & 0 & 0 \\ 0 & 1 & 0 \\ 0 & 0 & 1 \end{bmatrix}.$$

[1] Such behaviour is called *shorting* a stock, and we do not allow it here.

To set this up in R, we note first that the maximization problem is equivalent to minimizing the negative of the objective function, subject to the same constraints. This fact enables us to employ `solve.QP()`.

```
> A <- cbind(rep(1, 3), diag(rep(1, 3)))
> D <- matrix(c(0.01, 0.002, 0.002, 0.002, 0.01, 0.002, 0.002, 0.002, 0.01),
+              nrow=3)
> x <- c(0.002, 0.005, 0.01)
> b <- c(1, 0, 0, 0)
> # meq specifies the number of equality constraints;
> # these are listed before the inequality constraints
> solve.QP(2 * D, x, A, b, meq=1)
$solution
[1] 0.1041667 0.2916667 0.6041667

$value
[1] -0.002020833

$unconstrained.solution
[1] -0.02678571  0.16071429  0.47321429

$iterations
[1] 2 0

$iact
[1] 1
```

The optimal investment strategy (for this investor) is to put 10.4% of her fortune into the first stock, 29.2% into the second stock, and 60.4% into the third stock.

The optimal value of the portfolio is 0.0020 (from `$value` above). (Recall that the negative sign appears in the output, because we were minimizing the negative of the objective function.)

Exercises

1 (a) Find nonnegative x_1, x_2, x_3, and x_4 to minimize

$$C(x) = x_1 + 3x_2 + 4x_3 + x_4,$$

subject to the constraints

$$x_1 - 2x_2 \geq 9$$
$$3x_2 + x_3 \geq 9,$$

and

$$x_2 + x_4 \geq 10.$$

(b) Will the solution change if there is a requirement that any of the variables should be integers? Explain.

(c) Suppose the objective function is changed to

$$C(x) = x_1 - 3x_2 + 4x_3 + x_4.$$

What happens to the solution now?

2 Find nonnegative x_1, x_2, x_3, and x_4 to maximize

$$C(x) = x_1 + 3x_2 + 4x_3 + x_4,$$

subject to the constraints

$$x_1 - 2x_2 \leq 9$$
$$3x_2 + x_3 \leq 9,$$

and

$$x_2 + x_4 \leq 10.$$

Chapter exercises

1 Consider the data of Example 7.12. Calculate the slope and intercept for a line of "best-fit" for these data for which the intercept is at least as large as the slope.

2 Re-do the calculation in the portfolio allocation example using $k = 1$. How does being less risk-averse affect the investor's behavior?

3 Often, there are upper bounds on the proportion that can be invested in a particular stock. Re-do the portfolio allocation problem with the requirement that no more than 50% of the investor's fortune can be tied up in any one stock.

4 Duncan's Donuts Inc. (DDI) and John's Jeans Ltd. (JJL) are two stocks with mean daily returns of 0.005 and 0.010, respectively. What is the optimal portfolio for a completely risk-loving investor (i.e. risk-tolerance constant $k = 0$) who invests only in these two stocks? (Hint: this question does not require any computations.)

5 Suppose the daily returns for DDI and JJL are independent, but $\sigma_{DDI}^2 = 0.01$ and $\sigma_{JJL}^2 = 0.04$. What is the optimal allocation for an investor with a risk tolerance constant (a) $k = 1$? (b) $k = 2$? You can use the fact that

$$D = \begin{bmatrix} 0.01 & 0 \\ 0 & 0.04 \end{bmatrix}.$$

6 Repeat the preceding question under the assumption that the covariance between the returns for DDI and JJL is 0.01. You can use the fact that

$$D = \begin{bmatrix} 0.01 & 0.01 \\ 0.01 & 0.04 \end{bmatrix}.$$

Appendix

Review of random variables and distributions

Suppose an experiment is conducted in which a number of different outcomes are possible. Each outcome has a certain probability of occurrence.

Consider a cancer treatment that will be tested on 10 patients. The number of patients who show an increase in their white-blood cell count at the end of 5 weeks of treatment cannot be predicted exactly at the beginning of the trial, so this number, which we might label N, is thought of as a *random variable*. N is an example of a *discrete* random variable since it only takes values from a discrete set, i.e. $\{0, 1, 2, \ldots, 10\}$. The time, T, until death could also be measured for one of the patients; again, T cannot be predicted exactly in advance, so it is also an example of a random variable; since it can take a continuum of possible values, it is referred to as a *continuous* random variable.

A random variable is characterized by its distribution. This specifies the probability that the variable will take one or more values. If X denotes the number of heads obtained in two independent tosses of a fair coin, we might write

$$P(X \leq 1) = 0.75$$

to indicate that the probability of 0 or 1 head in two tosses is 0.75. In general, the function

$$F(x) = P(X \leq x)$$

is called the distribution function of the random variable X. If $F(x)$ has a derivative, we can define the probability density function of X as

$$f(x) = F'(x).$$

This is often possible with continuous random variables X. Note that, in this case,

$$F(y) = \int_{-\infty}^{y} f(x) \, dx.$$

Among other things, note that the area under the curve specified by $f(x)$ is 1.

The expected value of a random variable is also an important concept. For continuous random variables, we can write

$$E[X] = \int_{-\infty}^{\infty} x f(x)\, dx.$$

This is the mean value of the density function $f(x)$. It is often denoted by the symbol μ. We also can take expectations of functions of random variables using the formula

$$E[g(X)] = \int_{-\infty}^{\infty} g(x) f(x)\, dx.$$

An important example of this is the variance. The variance of a random variable gives an indication of the unpredictability in a random variable. Its formula is

$$\text{Var}(X) = E[(X - \mu)^2] = \int_{-\infty}^{\infty} (x - \mu)^2 f(x)\, dx.$$

Another important concept is that of *quantile*: this is the value of x for which $F(x)$ takes on a particular value. When the inverse function $F^{-1}(y)$ is defined, the α quantile of X is given by $F^{-1}(\alpha)$. For example, the 0.95 quantile is the value of x for which $F(x) = 0.95$; in other words, x is the 95th percentile of the distribution. Frequently used quantiles are the median $\tilde{x}$ which satisfies $F(\tilde{x}) = 0.5$, and the upper and lower quartiles which satisfy $F(x) = 0.75$ and $F(x) = 0.25$, respectively.

The following tables summarize properties of some commonly used univariate distributions:

Distribution name	$f(x)$	$F(x)$	$E[X]$	$\text{Var}(X)$
Uniform (a, b)	$\frac{1}{b-a}$, $a < x < b$	x	$\frac{a+b}{2}$	$\frac{(b-a)^2}{12}$
Exponential (λ)	$\lambda e^{-\lambda x}$, $x > 0$	$1 - e^{-\lambda x}$	$\frac{1}{\lambda}$	$\frac{1}{\lambda^2}$
Normal (μ, σ^2)	$\frac{1}{\sigma\sqrt{2\pi}} e^{-\frac{(x-\mu)^2}{2\sigma^2}}$	$\int_{-\infty}^{x} \frac{1}{\sigma\sqrt{2\pi}} e^{-\frac{(y-\mu)^2}{2\sigma^2}}\, dy$	μ	σ^2

Distribution name	$P(X = x)$	$E[X]$	$\text{Var}(X)$
Binomial (n, p)	$\binom{n}{x} p^x (1-p)^{n-x}$	np	$np(1-p)$
Poisson (λ)	$\frac{\lambda^x e^{-\lambda}}{x!}$	λ	λ

We conclude this review with some brief comments about bivariate distributions. In particular, suppose X and Y are continuous random variables having joint probability density $f(x, y)$. We can define expectations using double integrals:

$$E[g(X, Y)] = \int_{-\infty}^{\infty} \int_{-\infty}^{\infty} g(x, y) f(x, y) \, dx \, dy$$

for functions $g(x, y)$. In particular, setting $g(X, Y) = I(X \leq u)I(Y \leq v)$ gives

$$E[I(X \leq u)I(Y \leq v)] = \int_{-\infty}^{u} \int_{-\infty}^{v} f(x, y) \, dx \, dy,$$

which implies that, for any u and v,

$$P(X \leq u, Y \leq v) = \int_{-\infty}^{u} \int_{-\infty}^{v} f(x, y) \, dx \, dy.$$

Here, $I()$ denotes the indicator function which takes on the value 1, when its argument is true, and 0, when its argument is false.

The marginal density of X is obtained by integrating over all values of y:

$$f_X(x) = \int_{-\infty}^{\infty} f(x, y) \, dy,$$

and similarly, the marginal density of Y is obtained by integrating over all values of x:

$$f_Y(y) = \int_{-\infty}^{\infty} f(x, y) \, dx.$$

X and Y are stochastically independent if

$$f(x, y) = f_X(x) f_Y(y).$$

Among other things, this implies that $P(X \leq u, Y \leq v) = P(X \leq u)$ $P(Y \leq v)$, and, by the definition of *conditional probability*,

$$P(X \leq u | Y \leq v) = \frac{P(X \leq u, Y \leq v)}{P(Y \leq v)} = P(X \leq u).$$

The term on the left denotes the conditional probability that $X \leq u$, given that $Y \leq v$. Intuitively, the above statement means that knowledge of the value of Y does not give us any additional information with which to predict the value of X.

Index

...nes & Noble
Princeton, NJ
Tue 5 Oct 2010
$ 47.99 list
$ 43.19 after 10% discount
$ 3.02 tax
$ 46.21 total